The Power of a
PRAYING®
HUSBAND

STORMIE
OMARTIAN

HARVEST HOUSE PUBLISHERS

EUGENE, OREGON

THE POWER OF A PRAYING® HUSBAND
Copyright © 2001 Stormie Omartian
Published by Harvest House Publishers
Eugene, Oregon 97402
www.harvesthousepublishers.com

The Library of Congress has cataloged the edition as follows:

Omartian, Stormie.
    The power of a praying husband / Stormie Omartian.
        p. cm.
    ISBN 978-0-7369-1976-0
    1. Husbands—Religious life. 2. Prayer. I. Title.

BV4528.2 .O48 2001
248.8'425—dc21   2001024262

The 1687 Foundation Second Printing, 2012

Printed in the United States of America
Cover design by StandingPixels.com and Kristin Paul Designs

This book made available without charge by The 1687 Foundation, a nonprofit, tax-exempt organization dedicated to advancing spiritual and charitable purposes. Please note that these books may only be given away. They cannot be sold, cannot be used to raise money, and cannot be a "free giveaway" for any commercial or personal-gain purpose whatsoever.

For additional information, please contact:
Email: info@1687foundation.com
Tel: 541.549.7600
Fax: 541.549.7603

THE POWER OF A PRAYING HUSBAND

MILITARY EDITION
INTRODUCTION

by
Stormie Omartian

As I am sure you well know, one of the greatest challenges to any marriage where one or both people are in the military are the long separations. Whether it is the *husband* serving, or the *wife*, or in some cases *both* who are serving in the military, lengthy separations, along with the challenges of such uniquely demanding and dangerous work, can bring stress to even the strongest of marriages. But when a husband prays for his wife, he not only gets closer to God, he also gets closer to *her*, no matter how far the two of them are separated by time and space.

A few years ago, a group of military men serving in Iraq wrote to ask if I would send them copies of this book you are now holding. They were on a long deployment and wanted to stay in close contact with their wives. I was more than happy to send them my books. Not long after that, I received a thank-you letter and a group photo showing each of the men in the group holding his own copy of the book. That photo is one of my most treasured possessions. Knowing that these brave men would take time out of their demanding schedule to pray for their wives is deeply touching to me. I also know how much it meant to each of the wives. (That photo is on my website at www.StormieOmartian.com if you want to see it.)

My nephew recently left for his second year-plus deployment to Iraq, leaving his wife, their 18-month-old child, and a baby on the way. Through them I have seen the tremendous sacrifice military families have to make. That's why I extend this book to you with heartfelt thanks for all you and your wife do for us and for our country. You are our heroes.

—Stormie Omartian

*This book is dedicated to my husband,
Michael, whose every prayer for me I have
appreciated and benefited from far more
than words can describe.*

Contents

Acknowledgments

With special thanks:

✦ To the many faithful praying husbands who told me about the joys of seeing their prayers answered for their wives. Especially to Pastor Jack Hayford, Bishop Kenneth C. Ulmer, Bishop Eddie L. Long, Neil Anderson, James Robison, Michael Harriton, Mike Goldstone, Rodney Johnson, and Steven Curtis Chapman for your stories of answered prayer that you contributed to this book. I hold each of you in highest esteem for the kind of husbands, fathers, and men of God that you are.

✦ To the hundreds of praying wives who shared with me the ways they longed to have their husbands pray for them.

✦ To Susan Martinez, my secretary, life manager, sister, and friend, without whom I would never make a single deadline.

✦ To my husband, Michael, for cooking all those great dinners and praying for me to be able to hear God as I wrote this book.

✦ To my daughter, Amanda, for all the meals cooked, errands run, and rooms cleaned so I could have time to work.

✦ To my prayer partners Susan Martinez, Roz Thompson, Katie Stewart, Donna Summer, Bruce Sudano, Michael and Terry Harriton, and Tom and Patti Brussat, without whose prayers I would not have survived this year, let alone written a book.

✦ To my Harvest House family, especially Bob Hawkins Jr., Carolyn McCready, Julie McKinney, Teresa Evenson, Terry Glaspey, Betty Fletcher, LaRae Weikert, Barb Sherrill, and Peggy Wright, for all your prayers, e-mails, letters, calls, and support.

A Word from Michael

L et's face it, men, by the time we marry we bring many years of experiences, habits, personality traits, memories, preconceived notions, and personal ambitions with us into the marriage. Suddenly we are joined, for a lifetime, with a mate who has also brought many years of experiences, habits, personality traits, memories, preconceived notions, and personal ambitions into the marriage with her. We are faced with the need to communicate, compromise, submit to one another, and be unselfish. A tall order, to be sure. Either God has a tremendous sense of humor, or a desire to keep us continually growing. Probably both.

God intends each of our marriages to be a way for us to be totally fulfilled, but we have to live as an example of Christ's love for us. That's why a man's communication with his wife is dependent upon his communication with the Father. Praying specifically for our wives is a powerful thing. God is always listening. He considers every word. Yes, the God of all creation has His ear inclined toward us, and in Him we have the opportunity to defuse bombs the enemy has planted that are set to destroy what God has joined together.

Are there things about our wives we would like to see changed? Praying for those changes invites God to do great things in our lives. Without prayer, the success of our marriages depends on our own wisdom and effort. But what a resource for success awaits us when we pray! We see not only answers to our prayers for our wives, but things happen in us as well.

Throughout my marriage to Stormie I have witnessed miraculous answers to prayer—everything from seeing bondage from her damaged past broken in her, to the saving of her life in a medical emergency, to the flourishing of her ministry as an author. The more I understand how my wife benefits directly from my prayers for her, the more I understand how God uses those prayers to build my faith and how He changes and blesses me in the process.

It is with this confidence in God's answering the prayers of a husband for a wife that I recommend this book to you. And I know you'll enjoy it, because I have been praying for my wife as she writes it.

Michael Omartian

He who finds a wife finds a good thing,
And obtains favor from the LORD.

Proverbs 18:22

THE POWER

Thank you, sir, for reading this book. I'm sure that no one is holding a gun to your head to make you do it, but if she is, tell her to put it down because you intend to keep going.

I don't want to be presumptuous in any way, but I believe it is quite possible that you fit into one of the following categories. See if any of these are true about you:

1. You found this book mysteriously placed on the seat of your favorite chair, on the floor next to the commode, on the pillow on your side of the bed, inside your briefcase or lunch box or toolbox, on the front seat of the vehicle you drive to work, or on top of your desk, worktable, or TV remote.

2. Your praying wife bought this book for you so that you would never again have to feel guilty about not praying enough for her.

3. You bought this book yourself because you've wanted to pray effectively for your wife, but you didn't know where to begin.

4. You have longed to see meaningful and lasting changes happen in your wife, yourself, and your marriage, and you're hoping this book will help.

5. You are already a kind, thoughtful, loving, praying husband, and you want to always be learning new and effective ways to further bless your wife.
6. A friend recommended this book, and although you're skeptical, you're willing to give it a try to see if anything will come of it.
7. Your life has been threatened, and reading this book seems like a small price to pay in order to preserve it.

Whatever the case may be, I salute you, I commend you. You are a giant among men. I say to you that your efforts in reading this book will be well spent, your time will not be wasted, and you will find great rewards ahead.

WHY HER AND NOT HIM?

You may be asking yourself at this very moment, *Why isn't Stormie's husband writing this book?* The answer is simple. He's just like you. He is a busy man, with places to go, people to see, work to do, a family to support, food to eat, a life to live, golf to play, ball games to watch, channels to flip, and a chronic lack of patience when it comes to writing. It's not that he doesn't pray. He does. It's just that he is a man of few words when it comes to prayer. (Quite opposite of the way he is when the Chicago Cubs are losing.) In fact, he has always had one direct response to people who ask him, "Why don't you write a book called *The Power of a Praying Husband?*"

"If I wrote it," he says matter-of-factly, "it would be a brochure."

Double-spaced.

With lots of pictures.

The brochure part doesn't really bother me. Brevity isn't the issue as long as I know he is praying. The truth is, a husband's prayers for his wife don't have to be long and detailed. Short and to-the-point prayers are also powerful. That's because God has given the husband authority in the spirit realm that is unequaled. Whether or not his prayers are answered, however, depends on how that authority is handled. (More about that in the next chapter.)

With the success of my book *The Power of a Praying Wife*, I was afforded the opportunity to travel the country speaking to thousands of women and talking one-on-one with hundreds of them in each city I visited. I heard about their deep longings to have better relationships with their husbands and to see their marriages work successfully and become a source of fulfillment and joy for all concerned. The encouraging part to me was that these wives had found great answers to prayer when they had learned to pray for their husbands the way God wanted them to.

In letters and in person, I was asked countless times by these women to write *The Power of a Praying Husband*. I didn't seriously consider doing it until men started bringing up the same question.

"When are you going to write *The Power of a Praying Husband?*" many of the husbands would ask me.

"Would you actually read it if I wrote it?" I always asked them in return.

"Yes, definitely!" each one of them responded strongly. "I *want* to pray for my wife, I just don't know how."

I was surprised at the consistency of their responses and deeply touched by the honesty and sincerity with which they were spoken.

When I told my husband, Michael, about this repeated request from so many husbands as well as from the praying wives, without even taking his eyes off the TV he immediately suggested that *I* should write the book.

"Do you think maybe *you* should write it?" I asked him. His eyes glazed over and he gave me that same look I see every time I ask him if he wants to go shopping with me.

"No, you're the writer. I'm a musician," he said with finality, using the characteristically few words he spends on a subject he doesn't want to pursue—especially when he's in the middle of watching a game on television.

"GO, GO, GO, GO, GO," he screamed as he leaped up off the couch.

I was about to leave the room to begin writing immediately when I realized he hadn't been shouting at me, but instead at one of the Chicago Cubs who had just made it to first base.

"What about you writing the foreword then?" I probed further after he sat back down.

"Yes, definitely," he answered while riveted to the screen. "WAIT, NO, NO NO! YOU IDIOT."

I wasn't sure how to respond.

Then turning to me he explained, "This umpire is an idiot! That guy was safe!"

Feeling great relief that his character analysis wasn't a commentary on *me,* I pursued the conversation further.

"In that case," I continued, "can you give me a list of all the times you can remember when you prayed for me and God answered your prayers?"

"Not now," he protested. "I'll do it between the seventh and eighth innings."

"I meant sometime in the next few *months,*" I slowly explained.

"YEAH! YEAH! GOOD! GOOD!" he screamed at the top of his lungs, then looking at me said, "Did you say something?"

"Yes. Would you pray for me as I write this book?"

"Not now. Between the seventh and eighth innings."

"I meant throughout this year."

"Uh-huh."

"Is that a firm uh-huh?" I asked.

"Uh-huh," he replied.

So with my husband's enthusiastic endorsement and the encouragement of many husbands and wives, I have been unanimously elected to bring this book to you. I don't take this vote of confidence lightly. And even though my husband declined to write it, he did say he would be more than happy to orchestrate it if it were ever made into a musical.

ANOTHER GOOD REASON
TO READ THIS BOOK

When I asked God whether I was really the one to write this book or not, I received some interesting insight. I believe one of the main reasons the Lord wants *me* to write it is that there are ways I am suggesting you pray for your wife that might be viewed as self-serving or selfish if a man were to write them. But I'm inviting you to pray in these ways because I know it will be to your wife's greatest blessing as well as your own.

Also, as I thought about how many husbands had asked me to write this book, I began to see that, if I were taking a poll like they do during political campaigns, I could assume that the men I talked to were a good representation of *all* men. This means that my poll reflects *your* thoughts on the subject. Therefore, I'm sure you can see as well as I do that *THIS BOOK IS ACTUALLY YOUR IDEA!*

THE WAY WE WERE

During the first half of the 28 years Michael and I have been married, we experienced great strife and misery because we tried to do things in the flesh and not in the spirit. We each wanted the other to be a certain way, and we tried to *make* that happen ourselves instead of relying on the power of God to accomplish it. Our methods of forcing things to happen brought far less than satisfying results. Michael used anger as a weapon to control our lives, and I reacted to it by retreating mentally and emotionally.

Of course I had my favorite three-word prayer that I always prayed about the situation. You know the one. It's the "Change him, Lord!" prayer. But God never answered that prayer. Not even once. Then during a time of great strife between us, when I couldn't bear it anymore, I cried out to the Lord desperately for help. And God impressed upon my heart that, if I would be willing to lay down my life in prayer for Michael, He would use me to help Michael become all God had made him to be. In order to do that, however, I had to let God give me a new heart and begin to see Michael from God's perspective. When I consented to that and learned to pray for Michael in the manner God was showing me, I began to understand the source of his misplaced anger.

Michael was raised by a mother who was overbearing, controlling, and too strict with him. She had expectations of him far beyond his capabilities, inclinations, giftings, or the call of God upon his life. She wanted an A student. He was an undiagnosed dyslexic. She wanted a doctor. He was a musician. She wanted success. He struggled in school. She didn't understand his problem. He didn't understand it either.

Whether it was fair or not, there was a good explanation for his mother's attitude toward him. Her family had lived in Armenia, where most of them had been killed by the brutally oppressive Turkish army. Her own mother, Michael's grandmother, had been forced to watch her children be tortured and murdered right in front of her, a situation so horrendous that I can't even bring myself to write out the details for you here. After the slaughter of her family, Michael's grandmother escaped to America and eventually started a new family, into which Michael's mother was born.

The terrifying memories of what had happened, and the dangers and consequences of being poor, uneducated, and part of a minority in a hostile country, permanently marked the heart of Michael's grandmother and ultimately his mother's as well. They believed it was crucial to study diligently and work hard to ensure that this kind of devastation would never happen again. As a result, any member of the family who didn't do well was an embarrassment. Being a musician was even worse since it was not considered a real job that had any kind of real future.

The struggles of the Depression only added to Michael's mother's fears. As she was raising him in the years after that time, she would speak in terms of "survival," "security," "diligence," "accomplishments," and "excellence." She didn't understand words like "learning disability," "artistic temperament," "musical giftedness," or "unique calling of God." She thought he was being difficult and uncooperative. But he was just being who he was, all the while struggling with the belief that it wasn't enough.

I know all this is true because Michael's mother told me so. I became close to her in the months prior to our marriage, and I adored her. She became the mother I never had for that brief time before the ravages of cancer took her life less than a year later. Her struggle to survive had dramatically changed her perspective. She shared that with me too.

"I was way too hard on him," she said to me one day shortly after Michael and I were married. "I see now the mistakes I've made. Facing death makes you understand what is really important. I believe Michael suffers with anger and depression because of the way I was with him."

"Nobody understood those things back then," I tried to comfort her. "You were only doing what you thought was best."

"No, I pushed him way too far. I was overcritical. I expected too much," she answered, and proceeded to tell the same story Michael had told me before we were married.

Because Michael was raised under pressure to be what his mother expected him to be, he was always painfully aware of his inability to meet those expectations. As a result, when he was 19 he had a nervous breakdown. He had been attending college full-time during the day, which is pressure enough for someone with dyslexia, but in addition to that he was working full-time as a musician in clubs at night. The pressure became too much for him to bear. His mother took him to their family doctor, who made the decision to put Michael in a mental hospital because it was near to both the doctor's office and the family's home. He believed it would be a good place for Michael to rest and be medically treated for nervous exhaustion.

"The mental hospital was a big mistake," his mother said to me with tears in her eyes. "He didn't have anything wrong with him that required that type of facility, and yet he was locked in a place where he observed the horrifying actions of those who did need it. The experience did more to damage Michael than it did to help him."

The night before Michael went into the hospital, his cousin led him to receive the Lord. But even though he was then a believer, he still had little spiritual understanding. As a result, his experience in the mental hospital was extremely frightening to him. He thought there might be more wrong with him than there actually was. So what Michael carried with him *out* of that hospital a few weeks later was fear. One of his greatest fears was that he might end up in a mental hospital again. Even 15 years into our marriage, he would still have moments when, overtired and pressured, he would experience anxiety and depression about that very issue.

"The doctor himself later apologized to me," his mother said sadly. "He told me he believed it had been a mistake to put Michael in the mental hospital. I know he was right, because Michael experienced great depression and anxiety from that time on."

All that his mother shared helped me to understand the source of Michael's anger. It even opened my eyes to why he took his anger and resentment toward his mother out on me. He was angry at her, and I was guilty by association. But I was not able to take it very well because of my own past.

I was raised by an abusive mother who was mentally ill and who locked me in a closet for much of my early childhood. Because of this I was filled with fear, depression, hopelessness, and anxiety even into adulthood. I grew up feeling like a failure because my mother repeatedly told me I would be. Her rejection of me made me supersensitive to anything Michael did that also seemed like rejection. Because of the insecurities I brought into the marriage, his harsh words would devastate me, and I would react by withdrawing from him. I viewed him as someone I couldn't trust with my heart because I never knew when he was going to stab it with the knife of criticism or judgment.

When the pain in my marriage became too much for me to bear, I considered separation and divorce. It was at this point God told me that, if I would surrender my desire to escape and submit to His desire to make me an intercessor for Michael, then God would use me as an instrument of deliverance for him. If I would pray for him the way God instructed me to—which required a major change of heart on my part—God would answer my prayers. What I learned over the following years became the basis for my book *The Power of a Praying Wife*.

Even though I desired to do what God wanted, I still asked Him, "Why am *I* the only one who has to change? Doesn't Michael need change too?"

But God spoke to my heart, saying, "It's not a matter of who *needs* to change, it's a matter of who is *willing* to change. If you're willing to change, I can work through you right now."

I don't know if I was all that willing to change, but I *was* willing to do what God wanted me to do. And so I said "yes" to what He was asking of me. And from the time I began to pray for Michael from a right heart and in the way God was directing me to, I started to see changes in him. He became less and less angry. He began to gain a perspective on his past that he hadn't had previously.

"I believe that if my father had covered us spiritually the way he should have, things would have been very different for our whole family," Michael said to me one day. "My dad was a faithful father and husband, and he supported the family financially, but he didn't have much input into my life. I knew he loved me. He wasn't an ogre or anything, he was just very passive. He never took any active interest in who I was. For years I wasn't able to see the situation from my mother's perspective, but now I have new compassion for her. She had to do everything on her own. She had to carry so much weight in the family. He didn't cover her spiritually. There wasn't a balance in the house. She got cancer at 44 and died when she was barely 50, and I believe that was part of what ended up killing her."

This realization has been instrumental in helping Michael to see the importance of praying for his own family. It has motivated him to pray for me. And I know I owe much of the success of my life to his prayers.

THE POWER AND AUTHORITY

The power of a praying husband is not a means of gaining control over your wife. We all know that never really happens anyway. That's because God doesn't want us controlling other people. He wants us to let *Him* control *us*. When we humble ourselves before God and let *Him* control *us*, then He can work through us. God wants to work through you as an instrument of *His* power as you intercede for your wife.

The power in your prayer is God's. When you pray for your wife, you are inviting God to exercise His power in her life. Your prayer enables her to better hear God's voice and respond to God's leading. In spite of that, however,

God will never override a person's strong will. If anyone is determined to live outside of God's will, He will let that person do it. So, although your prayers have the potential to be powerful in your wife's life, there is a limit to what they can accomplish if *her* will—or *your* will—is opposed to the will of *God*. "Now this is the confidence that we have in Him, that if we ask anything according to His will, He hears us" (1 John 5:14).

God wants us to pray about all things, but He wants us to pray according to His will. That's why it's important to ask God to reveal His will to you and help you pray accordingly. Once you have the mind of God as to how to pray, it's easier to pray fervently and persistently. Just as we can't force our spouses to do what we want them to do, we can't force God to do our bidding either. It's *His* will, not ours that will be done.

Your spiritual authority with regard to your wife and family is unequaled. Because your spiritual authority comes from God, it must be used the way God intended. It must be motivated by his love and have His glory in mind. All God-given spiritual authority has as its foundation a humility that desires to serve God more than to control others. God wants you to serve Him by exerting your authority over the enemy. You have been given authority "over all the power of the enemy" (Luke 10:19), and you can devastate His plans on your wife's behalf. If you see the enemy creeping into your marriage in any way, stand up and boldly say:

"I will not permit any plans of the enemy to prevail in our marriage."

"I will not allow the enemy to drive a wedge between us."

"I will not stand by and see my wife deceived by lies of the enemy."

"I will not allow the enemy to attack my wife in any way."

"I will not allow miscommunication to rule our relationship."

"I will not permit the mistakes of our past, even yesterday's, to control our future."

Then pray, pray, pray. Because when you pray, no weapon formed against her or you will prosper (Isaiah 54:17).

DON'T LEAVE YOUR MARRIAGE
TO CHANCE

Remember the Scripture you read in the very beginning of the book? It says that God has already given you favor simply because you have a wife (Proverbs 18:22). There are certain blessings God has for you just because you are married. That's because God has declared the two of you to be one in His sight (Matthew 19:4-6). This means that what happens to one of you will affect the other. If she is happy, you will be happy. If you are blessed, she will be blessed. And of course the reverse is also true. If she is not happy, you definitely won't be either. Her problems are your problems, just as your problems are hers. That's why *your* prayers for her are so crucial. They will affect you both.

Whatever you don't pray about in your life you leave up to chance. And that's not good enough when it comes to your marriage.

The problem with chance in a marriage is, chances are there will be some difficult times. Chances are there will be disagreements. Chances are there will be misunderstandings and hurts. Chances are there will be selfishness and hardness of heart. That's because we are, after all, human. But if we leave the outcome of these things up to chance, we will wind up in trouble down the line. However, all of these things can be turned around through prayer.

If busyness, workaholism, unforgiveness, strife, child-rearing, careers, separate interests, boredom, or miscommunication has crept in between you and your wife, God can work through your prayers to bring down the wall that separates you, melt the armor that has been put on for self-protection, and mold you together in unity. It will give you a vision of hope for how God can redeem, restore, and make things right. Praying for your wife will not only soften her heart, but it will also soften yours as well.

You don't ever have to slip into marital deadness. Misery or divorce don't ever have to be your only two options. No matter what has happened between you, God can fix it. He is the God of wholeness and restoration. You have Him on your side. He has given you the power and the authority. Use them well.

HOW TO REALLY LOVE YOUR WIFE

Jesus said that the greatest act of love is to lay down your life for another (John 15:13). There are many ways to lay down your life for your wife without physically dying. One way is to lay down your life for her in prayer. It's sacrificing a relatively small amount of time for her greatest good, which is ultimately yours also.

There are many things a woman wants to hear from her husband. Three of the top four are probably "I love you," "You look beautiful," and "The bills are paid." But I know that one thing every woman wants to hear, the thing that will make her feel more loved than anything else, is "I'm praying for you today."

Whenever a wife hears that her husband is praying for her, it makes her feel loved and protected. It makes her feel she's important to him. If you want to see God soften your wife's heart, or make things right between you, or enrich your life together, or cause your marriage to run more smoothly, then pray for her. If you want your wife to throw herself at your feet, ask her, "How do you want me to pray for you today?" (Don't let me down here, ladies, I know you're reading this.) Okay, maybe that's overstating it a bit. But she will love you for it. Those words speak of your commitment to her and the marriage. Of course, if you tell her you're praying for her and you don't actually do it, I wouldn't go out in any lightning storms if I were you.

WHAT IF SHE'S NOT A BELIEVER?

Most women have a sense of their spiritual side—even those who have no professed religion or organized affiliation with a belief system. They have a recognition that there is a way of life that works and that it's wrapped up in the spiritual.

Prayer touches the heart of anyone for whom we pray. If your wife doesn't know the Lord, you can still pray all the prayers in this book for her and expect to see answers. The Bible says that "the unbelieving wife is sanctified by the husband" (1 Corinthians 7:14). You provide a covering over her. Of course, this doesn't substitute for her knowing the Lord, but it means that your prayers will have a positive and powerful effect on her. Just remember every time you pray for her, ask God to open her heart to the truth of His Word and give her a life-changing encounter with Him.

WHAT EACH CHAPTER HOLDS

Each of the 20 chapters in this book focuses on one area of prayer in a way I hope will be enlightening, encouraging, and motivating to you. I will share with you what I have learned from experience and what God has taught me. At the end of each chapter will be the following four sections:

1. She Says

   This is the result of a personal survey I made of hundreds of women all over America. I asked them how they wanted their husbands to pray for them. The amazing thing about this is that the results were the same in every city and state I traveled to!

2. He Says

   This is what a number of individual husbands said about how they pray for their wives and about the answers they have seen to their prayers. I was encouraged, amused, touched, and enlightened by their words, and I know you will be too.

3. Prayer Power

   This is a suggested prayer on the subject of that chapter. You can pray it as it is, or include anything personal you want to add. It's there as a guide for you.

4. Power Tools

   This page contains verses from the Bible that lend support to that area of prayer, which will be of great help to you as you pray in depth about it. You can speak these out loud in a declaration of truth over your situation or pray them over your wife.

ONE PRAYER AT A TIME

Don't be overwhelmed by the many ways to pray for your wife. Simply take it one day and one prayer at a time. You can pray through a different chapter each day, or concentrate on praying one each week. I'm not saying how much you should pray, but the Bible says that "he who sows sparingly will also reap sparingly, and he who sows bountifully will also reap bountifully" (2 Corinthians 9:6). The more you pray, the more benefits you will reap. If you want to make room for God to bring about big changes quickly in your wife, yourself, and your marriage, try praying one of these chapters each day for several weeks. See if something good doesn't start happening in your heart and in hers.

Sometimes I have been asked, "Does it really work to pray prayers that someone else has written? In order to truly pray from the heart, shouldn't you make up your own prayers?" My answer to that is, "Does it really work to sing praise songs that someone else has written?" I believe it does. It's good to make up your own praise song, and God delights in that, but the important thing is that what you're praying or singing resonates in your own heart. Is it a prayer that *you* would pray if *you* had thought of it? Do you believe it's a prayer God can answer? If the answer is yes to either of these questions, then that prayer has power. It doesn't matter who thought of it first.

Often when we pray for our mates, we pray about the most urgent need—which is right to do—but we neglect the "maintenance prayers." If you have a high-maintenance spouse, you definitely don't want to do that. Such prayers head off trouble before it happens. They put out small fires before they become roaring flames. Most of the prayers in this book are maintenance prayers. If you pray all of them for your wife a few times a year, you will keep your marriage healthy and enjoy a wife who is happy and fulfilled. They will remind you to pray in ways you might not have had time to think about.

Whether you pray the prayers I have suggested or pray your own, the bottom line is, keep praying and don't give up. Sometimes prayers are answered quickly, but many are not. Jesus said "Men always ought to pray and not lose heart" (Luke 18:1). Keep praying and you *will* see God answer. And don't worry about how the answers will be manifested. You don't have to make them happen. It's *your* job to pray. It's *God's* job to answer. Trust Him to do His job.

CHAPTER ONE

HER HUSBAND

I once saw a football game where the home team was losing and there were less than 15 seconds left in the game. They needed a touchdown to win, but everything was against them making a score in that amount of time. The game appeared to be over, and the opposing team and fans were already celebrating. Some people were even leaving the stadium. But the losing team and coach didn't give up or let their morale fall. Instead they pulled an unlikely play out of their book, and through the most astonishing sequence of events, the home team made a winning touchdown in the last few seconds of the game. It was so amazing that news reports of it even referred to it as a miracle.

Your marriage is like that football game. You and your wife are a team. And she wants the security of knowing that when things are tough and down to the wire—even when the enemy is already celebrating your demise and all appears to be lost—you have the faith to believe that up to the very last second everything can turn around. She needs the assurance you have a play in your pocket that can take you down the field with the ball for a possible winning score. She wants you to trust that with God nothing is impossible, and because of that you will never give up hoping for the impossible to happen.

When your wife knows you are praying, she is confident of all of these things.

In my survey of wives, 85 percent of them said the most important prayer their husband could pray was that he would become the man, husband, and head of the home God wanted him to be. This is the most important place for a man to begin praying.

"THAT YOUR PRAYERS MAY NOT BE HINDERED"

The good thing about prayer—or the problem with prayer, depending on your perspective—is that we have to go to God to do it. This means we can't get away with anything. It means that any negative thoughts, bad attitudes, hardness of heart, or selfish motives are going to be revealed by the Lord. Fervent and honest prayer causes the depths of our hearts to be exposed. That can be uncomfortable. Even downright miserable.

If there is one thing I have learned about prayer, it's that if we have any unforgiveness, bitterness, selfishness, pride, anger, irritation, or resentment in our hearts, our prayers will not be answered. "If I regard iniquity in my heart, the Lord will not hear" (Psalm 66:18). Our hearts have to be right when we pray. We all—men and women alike—jeopardize our own prayers when we don't pray them from a right heart.

What is in our hearts when we pray has more effect on whether our prayers are answered than the actual prayer itself. That's why, when we come before Him to pray, God asks us to first confess anything in our hearts that shouldn't be there. He does that so nothing will separate us from Him.

The Bible says, "Husbands, likewise, dwell with them *with understanding*, giving *honor* to the wife, as to the weaker vessel, and as being *heirs together* of the grace of life, that your *prayers may not be hindered*" (1 Peter 3:7).

Part of dwelling with your wife *with understanding* means recognizing that your wife is in need of your covering, protection, and love. And because you are *heirs together* of God's grace, you need to *honor* her in your thoughts, words, and actions. When you don't, your *prayers are hindered*. This means *all* of your prayers, not just those for your wife. Many men have not seen answers to their prayers because they have not learned this key step. One of the best ways to honor your wife is to pray for her from a heart that is clean before God.

Ask God to show you whatever you need to see about the condition of your heart. You may have the perfect marriage and be sublimely happy, and still be less than what God wants in your attitude toward your wife. Whatever He reveals, confess it to Him. Once we confess our less-than-perfect attitudes to the Lord, He helps us get beyond them. You'll find that the most difficult part about being a praying husband will not be the amount of time it takes to pray for your wife—rather, it will be praying with a heart that's right before God. That's why praying for your wife must begin with praying for yourself.

Don't worry, God taught this same principle to the praying wives. Many women told me that it was at this point in the chapter they threw the book across the room and said, "Forget it! I'm not doing that!" Of course the Holy Spirit wouldn't let them get away with that for long, and so they eventually picked the book back up and kept reading. So if you would like to throw this book across the room and say, "Forget it! I'm not doing that!" this would be a good time to do it. I know you'll pick it back up again, because you're going to get awfully tired of your prayers not being answered.

IT TAKES TWO TO MAKE ONE

When God created Adam, in spite of all the greatness that was in him God knew he still needed a companion, a helpmate who would fit with him, be a complement to him, and complete him (Genesis 2:18). So He created Eve. In spite of all the greatness that is in you, dear brother, God made your wife to be a complement to you and make you complete. You do the same for her.

God says that when you and your wife were married you became one flesh (Genesis 2:24). Isn't it amazing that we were created to be one with our mates? That feels possible when we start out. There is the *anticipation* of oneness in that first moment when you sense you were destined to be more than friends. There is the *sense* of oneness in the courtship. The *promise* of oneness in the engagement period. The *declaration* of oneness in the wedding vows. The *thrill* of oneness on the honeymoon. The *excitement* of oneness as a home is established. Then somewhere along the way, the oneness gets eroded by a subtle separateness.

How does that happen?

The answer is the world, the flesh, and the devil. The world creeps in, along with raising children, pursuing careers, and dealing with the busyness of life. We begin to find more fascination or distraction in *it* than we do in our mates. Our flesh takes over when we decide to be self-centered instead of self-sacrificing. Then there is Satan.

God created marriage at the beginning. Satan has been trying to destroy it ever since. You and your wife are created in God's image (Genesis 1:27). Satan wants to make you over into *his*. Satan doesn't want your marriage to succeed and has in fact set up a plan for its destruction. He is even now making plans to destroy your marriage. But you, my precious brother, have been given the power and authority to put a stop to this through your prayers. When you pray for your wife, it keeps the world at bay, it transforms selfish hearts, and it derails the devil's plans. If God has asked you to pray for your enemies, how much more does He want you to pray for the person you are supposed to love and with whom you have become one? But first you have to pray for *yourself*.

FIVE WAYS TO BE THE HUSBAND
GOD WANTS YOU TO BE

In the Bible, God commands, "All of you be of *one mind*, having *compassion* for one another; *love* as brothers, be *tenderhearted*, be *courteous*" (1 Peter 3:8). Paying heed to these five directives can change your life and your marriage and make you the man and husband God wants you to be. It's definitely something well worth praying about.

1. BE OF ONE MIND

It's horrible to have strife in a marriage. It makes us miserable. It affects every area of our lives. And it's probably the closest thing to hell we'll ever know on earth. If it goes on long enough, it can destroy everything. Jesus said, "Every kingdom divided against itself is brought to desolation, and every city or house divided against itself will not stand" (Matthew 12:25). Those are frightening predictions. But prayer is the key by which unity in the marriage relationship can be maintained.

A man and wife cannot live entirely independently of one another without paying a steep price for it. It makes them incomplete. "Neither is a man independent of woman, nor woman independent of man, in the Lord" (1 Corinthians 11:11). But because men and women are different, it's quite easy for them to get off onto completely separate paths. Even in the closest of marriages, the two partners are still not joined at the hip. You and your wife may have separate work, interests, and activities, but if you are praying with and for one another regularly, it will keep you in tune and on the same path. Without this unity of mind and spirit that prayer provides, it's too easy to get used to the other one not being there. And if resentment about that creeps into the heart of either one of you, you can begin to hold yourself apart from one another mentally, physically, or emotionally, without even realizing it.

It is especially important to be of the same faith and beliefs. In fact, this is a good place to begin praying. Your entire relationship is compromised if you are not on the same page in this area. For example, going to separate churches, or going to a church where one of you is not happy, or one of you going to church while the other one consistently does not, all promote a lack of unity.

If you can think of other issues such as this that have caused division between you and your wife, pray specifically about them. Ask God to change your heart where necessary to bring you into unity with your wife. Where your wife's attitude and perspective need to change, pray for her to be able to change them. Your marriage will be a strong force for good if the two of you are of one mind.

2. BE COMPASSIONATE

Have you ever seen your wife suffering, but you don't know what to do about it? Some men become impatient with that. Others feel so at a loss or overwhelmed by it that it causes them to withdraw. If you recognize that happening to you, ask God to give you a heart of compassion. To be compassionate toward your wife is to have a deep sympathy for any area in which she suffers and to have a strong desire to alleviate that suffering.

Part of being compassionate has to do with simply listening. That means being able to listen without having that faraway look in your eyes that says, "I have more important things to do. Let's get this over with quickly." Your wife is not expecting you to fix everything. She just needs to know that you hear her heart and care about how she feels.

In the past my husband would stand still and listen to me for no more than three seconds (I timed this) before he would walk out of the room. If I wanted him to hear a complete sentence, I either had to run after him or finish the sentence the next time I saw him. Even when I did get him to actually sit down and look at me while I was speaking, I still had to ask him to give me some indication that he comprehended what I was saying. Usually I said something like "Blink if you can hear me." When he blinked, it meant so much to know he had heard my voice. Now he has a heart for my struggles, and he listens with care. Those moments of listening and indicating compassion have been healing to our relationship.

Pray that God will give you a heart of compassion toward your wife and the patience to listen to her when she needs you to do so. It's a fine art worth cultivating. It can get you places with her where you've dreamed of being.

3. BE LOVING

Jesus loves us with fidelity, purity, constancy, and passion no matter how imperfect we are. If a man doesn't love his wife in that same way, he will abuse his authority and his headship and as a result will abuse *her*. Because you are one with your wife, you must treat her the way you would your own body. You wouldn't do anything to deliberately hurt or destroy it. You love it and care for it. "Let each one of you in particular so love his own wife as himself" (Ephesians 5:33).

Jack Hayford, our pastor for 23 years, always said he could tell when a woman was truly loved by her husband, because she grew more beautiful as the years went on. He recognized an inner beauty that doesn't fade, but rather increases with time when a woman is loved.

You have no idea how much your love means to your wife. Don't withhold it from her, or one way or another you will lose her. The Bible says, "Do not withhold good from those to whom it is due, when it is in the power of your hand to do so" (Proverbs 3:27). Ask God to increase your love for your wife and enable you to show it in a way that makes her beautiful.

4. BE TENDERHEARTED

Is there anything about your wife that bothers you? Is there something that she does or says, or *doesn't* do or say, that irritates you? Do you find yourself wanting to change something about her? What happens when you try to *make* those changes occur? How does she respond when you show your irritation? Have you ever just given up and said, "It's no use. She's never going to be any different"?

The truth is, we all have a hard time changing. Try as we may, we can't change ourselves in any significant way. Only God can make changes in us that last. Only *His* power can transform us. That's why prayer is a more tender and more certain way to see changes happen in your wife.

For example, does your wife always run late, while you like to be on time? She's probably not doing it on purpose. She may either be a poor judge of time or else she is trying to do too much. Pray that God will help her to organize things better or not take on more than she can handle, or that she will gain a clearer concept of time. Above all, don't let anger, harshness, or demeaning attitudes creep in. Criticism intended to make your wife change doesn't work. It will never give you the results you want. The only thing that works is prayer.

So rather than be impatient with your wife's weaknesses, ask God to give you a tender heart so you can pray for her about them. Ask Him to show you how they are a complement to your strengths. And remember that, though the ways you and your wife are the same can unite you, the ways you are different can keep things interesting.

5. BE COURTEOUS

Do you ever talk to your wife in a way that would be considered rude if you were speaking to a friend or business associate? Are you kind to everyone all day at work, but then you take out your frustration, exhaustion, and anger on your wife when you get home? Do you ever allow criticism of your wife to come out of your mouth in front of other people? If so, as a sister in the Lord who deeply cares about both you and your wife, allow me to give you your first serious assignment in this book:

STOP THAT!

Marriage is hard enough without one of the parties being rude, cruel, or inconsiderate. Nothing makes a marriage feel more like hell on earth. Nothing is more upsetting, defeating, tormenting, suffocating, or emotion-provoking, nothing does more to bring out the worst in us, than a marriage where one of the partners is lacking in common courtesy. I have heard of more marriages dissolving because the wife had been treated rudely for so long that she felt herself becoming resentful, angry, bitter, and hopeless. In other words, she was turning into the kind of person she never wanted to be. We have to care enough about our mates to stop doing things that hurt or upset them.

There is nothing more wonderful than the male voice. It is strong and deep and rich. And the sound of male voices singing together is one of the most beautiful sounds on earth. But the male voice can also be terrifying, especially to women and children. Most men have no idea about the power of their voice. When a man speaks, his words have the power to create and the power to destroy. His words can be like a sharp knife that wounds and kills, or a soothing balm that heals and brings life.

I'm not saying that you shouldn't talk honestly and openly with your wife about the issues in your lives. By all means, put your thoughts and feelings on the table. But don't let your words turn into weapons of criticism that destroy what you want to preserve. Even when we don't mean to, our impatience or exhaustion can make our words seem less than courteous. Remember that "the kingdom of God is not in word but in power" (1 Corinthians 4:20). It's not the words you speak, it's the power of God behind them that will make the difference. Praying first, *before* you talk about a sensitive subject, will give your words power and ensure that you speak them from a right heart.

Your wife was created as a gift from God to complete you. "Nor was man created for the woman, but woman for the man" (1 Corinthians 11:9). But she must be treated as the gift from God that she is, in order for that complete blessing to happen in your life. Your wife will prove to be your greatest asset if you value and honor her. The Bible tells us that "whatever we ask we receive from Him, because we keep His commandments and do those things that are pleasing in His sight" (1 John 3:22). Pray for God to help you speak to your wife in a courteous way that is pleasing in His sight, and to convict your heart when you do not.

Praying about these five simple biblical directives will transform your life and your marriage. And no matter how great your marriage is, God wants it to be better. Since God tells us to "be transformed," that must mean there is always room for improvement (Romans 12:2). Therefore it stands to reason that, as we improve individually, our marriages will also improve. Next to your love for her, the greatest gift you can give your wife is your own wholeness. Her most fervent desire for you is that you become the man God created you to be. It must be your desire also. God has given you strength, brilliance, power, authority, and the wonderful and admirable traits that come with being a man. Ask God to help you use them well and to His glory. Ask God to make you everything He created you to be so you and your wife will always be a winning team.

SHE SAYS...

Please pray for yourself that:

1. You will be the husband God wants you to be.
2. You will know how to really love your wife.
3. You will be led by the Holy Spirit in all decisions.
4. You will be delivered from negative behavior.
5. You will speak words that build and not destroy.
6. You will have the desire to pray for your wife.
7. You will grow spiritually, emotionally, and mentally.

HE SAYS...
BY MICHAEL OMARTIAN

Michael is a record producer and songwriter. He and Stormie have been married for 28 years, and they have three grown children.

I just heard the sad story of yet another woman who lived in a marriage where she had to endure the overbearing actions and declarations of her husband. It has ended in a divorce. It was a marriage in which her opinions were not valued or needed, and she was made to feel disrespected, unloved, powerless, and useless. The worst part is that such things are happening alarmingly often even in Christian marriages. The reality is that many men have been taught strange interpretations of portions of the Bible. These misinterpretations have been spread through ignorance and because of some men's need to feel powerful as the "priest" of the home. No wonder the feminists have had a field day.

Although some women have been hurt and damaged through the extremism of the women's liberation movement, I can certainly see how it got started. We men can do a much better job of loving our wives as Christ loved the church. I know *I* can, and I pray that I will. I believe that through prayer God will give us men the tools we need so we can regard our wives with great respect and affection and become the instruments of support that they need.

Christ died for the church. We need to ask God to help us rise to the standard He has for us so that we will consider our wives before ourselves. That way our marriages can be a very different story.

PRAYER POWER

Lord, create in *me* a clean heart and renew a right spirit within me (Psalm 51:10). Show me where my attitude and thoughts are not what You would have them to be, especially toward my wife. Convict me when I am being unforgiving. Help me to let go of any anger, so that confusion will not have a place in my mind. If there is behavior in me that needs to change, enable me to make changes that last. Whatever You reveal to me, I will confess to You as sin. Make me a man after Your own heart. Enable me to be the head of my home and family that You created me to be.

Lord, show me how to really cover (wife's name) in prayer. Enable me to dwell with her with understanding and give honor to her so that my prayers will not be hindered (1 Peter 3:7). Renew our love for one another. Heal any wounds that have caused a rift between us. Give me patience, understanding, and compassion. Help me to be loving, tenderhearted, and courteous to her just as You ask me in Your Word (1 Peter 3:8). Enable me to love her the way that You do.

Lord, I pray that You would bring (wife's name) and me to a new place of unity with one another. Make us be of the same mind. Show me what I need to do in order to make that come about. Give me words that heal, not wound. Fill my heart with Your love so that what overflows through my speech will be words that build up, not tear down. Convict my heart when I don't live Your way. Help me to be the man and husband that You want me to be.

POWER TOOLS

A MAN SHALL LEAVE HIS FATHER AND MOTHER AND BE JOINED TO HIS WIFE, AND THE TWO SHALL BECOME ONE FLESH...LET EACH ONE OF YOU IN PARTICULAR SO LOVE HIS OWN WIFE AS HIMSELF, AND LET THE WIFE SEE THAT SHE RESPECTS HER HUSBAND.

EPHESIANS 5:31,33

ONE WHO TURNS AWAY HIS EAR FROM HEARING THE LAW, EVEN HIS PRAYER IS AN ABOMINATION.

PROVERBS 28:9

HUSBANDS, LOVE YOUR WIVES, JUST AS CHRIST ALSO LOVED THE CHURCH AND GAVE HIMSELF FOR HER.

EPHESIANS 5:25

CONFESS YOUR TRESPASSES TO ONE ANOTHER, AND PRAY FOR ONE ANOTHER, THAT YOU MAY BE HEALED. THE EFFECTIVE, FERVENT PRAYER OF A RIGHTEOUS MAN AVAILS MUCH.

JAMES 5:16

HUSBANDS OUGHT TO LOVE THEIR OWN WIVES AS THEIR OWN BODIES; HE WHO LOVES HIS WIFE LOVES HIMSELF. FOR NO ONE EVER HATED HIS OWN FLESH, BUT NOURISHES AND CHERISHES IT, JUST AS THE LORD DOES THE CHURCH.

EPHESIANS 5:28,29

CHAPTER TWO

HER SPIRIT

Your wife is like an automobile. She may be high maintenance like an Italian sports car. She might be as refined and expensive as a German luxury sedan. She may be solid and sturdy like an SUV, or delicate like a Pebble Beach Concours d'Elegance show car. She could be an efficient six-cylinder type, or be a faster but costlier V-8 model. She may be dependable in all kinds of weather like a four-wheel drive, or she may have no downhill traction control at all, even on a good day. Whatever she is, whether she is tiny like a compact car or full-size and beyond, she needs fuel to make her run smoothly.

Your wife's spirit is the gas in her car. She may have the greatest chassis, a fine interior, fabulous sleek lines, an engine that purrs like a kitten, a wonderful back seat, a roomy trunk, a beautiful nose, and all the standard accessories, but if she doesn't have fuel then she's not going to run. Her exterior will still look good, but her power supply will be diminished And not only must her tank be full, but her battery needs to be charged, her oil kept clean, her brake fluid replenished, and yes, she must have a good supply of antifreeze for those cold nights.

Without the daily infilling of the Holy Spirit, we all run on empty. Your wife may be running on empty right now and not even realize it. Some women don't ever take time to check their gauges, so they're completely surprised when they suddenly run out of fuel. If a woman doesn't spend enough time every day with the Lord in prayer, worship, and the Word of God, she will lose ground, and the enemy of her soul will run her down.

Your wife may be too solid in the Word of God to doubt her salvation, or His promise of eternal life, or His grace and goodness. But Satan may be able to get her to doubt that God created her with valuable gifts and a calling of her own. Or there may be times when she questions whether all things really do work together for good. When she experiences these kinds of attacks, and all women do at one time or another, it will deplete her. Many women can get eroded physically, emotionally, and mentally by unrelenting attacks of the enemy and not even be aware that it's happening. And the effects of it will carry over into your marriage. Your wife's relationship with God will affect her relationship with you more than anything else.

Because you are the head of the home and have been given authority over "*all* the power of the enemy" (Luke 10:19), you can inform him that he cannot lie to your wife or twist the truth of God in her mind. You can pray that your wife will be so solid in the truth that she can immediately identify a lie of the enemy, cast it aside, and listen only to the voice of God.

In my survey of women, the number-one area in which women most want their husbands to pray for *them* is their spiritual walk. Your wife wants to be a strong woman of God. She desires a relationship with God that is solid, and faith that is unshakable. And because women feel pulled in so many directions, they need prayer for patience, love, peace, and all the other fruits of the spirit to be manifested in their lives.

Your wife also wants to know God's will and be certain she is in the center of it. Having clarity about what God is calling her to do, and then doing it, gives her peace. For example, if God is calling her at this time in her life to stay home and take care of her children, she needs to hear from God about it so that she will be satisfied to do that. Your prayers will help her hear from God and be content no matter what state she is in.

Another good reason to pray for your wife's spiritual walk is that it is far better if both of you are putting your expectations in God. That keeps you from putting all your expectations on each other and becoming disappointed when they are not met.

When your wife's tank is empty, her sound system will still work, and she may appear to be in good shape, but her wheels won't turn because she can't accelerate, let alone get up to full speed. Her steering will go out, so she can't navigate. Her brakes won't function, so she can't stop when she needs to. She must be filled afresh with the fuel of the Holy Spirit each day. She must be charged with the power of God. When her tank is full, she'll have automatic climate control, she'll be able to go the distance, and the ride will be smooth.

Does your wife have enough of what she needs for the distance she has to go today? Has she filled up with the finest? Ask God about this, and He will show you.

SHE SAYS...

Please pray for your wife that:

1. She will be strong in faith.
2. She will grow spiritually.
3. She will spend time in the Word and in prayer.
4. She will have discernment and revelation.
5. She will become a mighty woman of God.
6. She will be a light to others.
7. She will know God's will and live in it.

HE SAYS...
BY MICHAEL GOLDSTONE

Michael is the owner of a lighting distribution company. He and his wife, Debra, have been married for 28 years, and they have two grown children and one grandchild.

I have prayed for my wife nearly every day for many years now. Before we leave each other in the morning, I take her close to myself and cover her, both with my arms and with my prayers. It has been my high priority to give her all the time she needs to update me on all that is going on in her life—her health, her relationships, her ministry opportunities, and all of her feelings. So as I am holding her, I ask God to work in those specific areas that are most meaningful to her for that day. I pray for physical protection. And I pray that God would draw her close to Himself and that she would have a special sense of His presence that day.

It only takes a minute or two, but I have been consistent, by God's grace, in doing this daily for years. God has been faithful to answer my prayers, and it has given Deb tremendous comfort, support, and assurance of how much she is loved by me. We still feel like newlyweds in many respects—so excited to be with each other. I know prayer has a lot to do with that.

PRAYER POWER

Lord, as much as I love my wife, I know You love her more. I realize that I cannot meet her every need and expectation, but You can. I pray that You will give (<u>wife's name</u>) the fulfillment of knowing You in a deeper and richer way than she ever has before. Help her to be diligent and steadfast in her walk with You, never doubting or wavering. Make her strong in spirit and give her an ever-increasing faith that always believes that You will answer her prayers.

Help her to carve out time every day to spend with You in Your Word and in prayer and praise. May Your words abide in her, so that when she prays You will give her the desires of her heart (John 15:7). Help her to increase her knowledge of You. May she turn to You first for everything as You become her constant companion. Give her discernment and revelation and enable her to hear Your voice instructing her. Help her to stay focused on You, no matter how great the storm is around her, so that she never strays off the path You have for her. Keep me aware of when she needs a fresh filling of Your Spirit so that I will be prompted to pray.

It is the desire of her heart to be a godly example to her friends and family, so give her patience with everyone she encounters. Help her to be so filled with Your Spirit that people sense *Your* presence when they are in *her* presence. I know she wants to serve You, but help her to understand when to say no if she is being asked to do more than she should. May she glorify You in all she does.

Your Word says that whoever finds You finds life and obtains Your favor (Proverbs 8:35), so I pray that (<u>wife's name</u>) will find new life in You today and enjoy Your blessings poured out upon her. Guide her in everything she does, so that she becomes the dynamic, mighty woman of God You want her to be. Give her knowledge of Your will and enable her to stay in the center of it. Help her to trust You with all her heart and not depend on her own understanding. May she acknowledge You in all her ways (Proverbs 3:5,6).

POWER TOOLS

BLESSED ARE THOSE WHO HUNGER AND THIRST FOR RIGHTEOUSNESS, FOR THEY SHALL BE FILLED.

MATTHEW 5:6

IF YOU ABIDE IN ME, AND MY WORDS ABIDE IN YOU, YOU WILL ASK WHAT YOU DESIRE, AND IT SHALL BE DONE FOR YOU.

JOHN 15:7

WHOEVER DRINKS OF THE WATER THAT I SHALL GIVE HIM WILL NEVER THIRST. BUT THE WATER THAT I SHALL GIVE HIM WILL BECOME IN HIM A FOUNTAIN OF WATER SPRINGING UP INTO EVERLASTING LIFE.

JOHN 4:14

IF YOU HAVE FAITH AS A MUSTARD SEED, YOU WILL SAY TO THIS MOUNTAIN, "MOVE FROM HERE TO THERE," AND IT WILL MOVE; AND NOTHING WILL BE IMPOSSIBLE FOR YOU.

MATTHEW 17:20

GLORY IN HIS HOLY NAME; LET THE HEARTS OF THOSE REJOICE WHO SEEK THE LORD!

PSALM 105:3

CHAPTER THREE

HER EMOTIONS

Your wife's emotions can be compared to a finely crafted violin. When the instrument is perfectly tuned the result is beautiful music. But because the violin is so delicate and highly sensitive to its surroundings, it doesn't take much for it to be affected dramatically. Any change in temperature, humidity, or altitude—a change so subtle that it may be imperceptible to you—can send it horrifyingly off pitch. And it doesn't have to be out of tune very much to make everyone within listening range completely miserable.

When a violin is played, the end result can be beautiful, rich, deep, pleasurable music. Or it can be harsh, dissonant, screeching, nerve-jolting, cacophonous noise. Whether it is one or the other depends on the condition of the violin, of course, but mostly upon the proficiency of the one playing it. When your wife's emotions are in the hands of the enemy, everything gets out of tune and the results are unpleasant and upsetting. When God is in charge, her emotions are an asset and the end result is soothing.

I'm sure you are already well aware that your life can be dramatically affected by what your wife experiences in her emotions. If she is depressed, anxious, angry, or hurt, chances are you will feel it in some way too. Some men react to their wife's emotions by tuning out. They don't have a clue as to what is going on, so they withdraw and stop listening. Others may make light of what their wives are experiencing, in hopes of minimizing the effect. Then other men will turn up the volume of their lives, hoping to drown out these mysterious problems. But I don't believe men react this way because they don't care. It's because they don't know what to do about it—and that realization alone is overwhelming to them.

The best way to approach the matter of your wife's emotions is to ask God to give you insight into what your wife is feeling and show you how to pray accordingly. Much of what happens in a woman's emotions begins in her mind. The enemy of her soul will feed her thoughts that make her feel depressed, sad, angry, bitter, anxious, fearful, lonely, or full of self-doubt. He will make her think that such thoughts are reality, or that God is giving her revelation for her life. When the enemy screams lies and confusion at her, God will use your prayers to put an end to it and bring the silence, clarity, and peace she needs. Your prayers will clear her mind, calm her emotions, help her to see the truth, and make her better able to hear from God.

Our marriages would all be better if each of us were totally whole before we were married. But achieving wholeness can take a lifetime, and that's longer than most of us are willing to wait before we marry. However, often the very conditions we need for emotional healing are provided in the marriage itself. Emotional healing happens faster within the context of a committed, unconditional love relationship because the hurting person often feels safe enough to face the pain of the past. She doesn't have to try to hold it together, or keep up an image, or pretend there is no hurt.

If you found that after you were married a variety of hurts and emotions began to surface in your wife—things you had never been aware of before—rejoice that you have been deemed trustworthy enough to be her support through the healing time. Don't run from the task or be afraid of it. You are not required to be the healer, or to fix everything, or to have all the answers. Only God can heal damaged emotions, and He will do it from the inside out. But your prayers are crucial to keeping the devil at bay while that is being accomplished.

Because of my own emotional healing from the effects of child abuse (which I described in my book *Stormie*), I have often been asked certain questions by concerned husbands who are married to wives with deep emotional hurts. One man who was typical of many said, "I don't know what to do for my wife when she is depressed. What can I say? How can I help her? Nothing I do seems to make any difference."

I answered him this way.

"So much of what your wife is experiencing in her emotions is a result of things she has experienced in her past," I told him. "And it is hard for you to understand because you have not come out of that same background. But God wants to heal your wife's pain and give her emotional wholeness. He is allowing your wife to go through all this now *because* she is married to you. It's happening because *you* are providing a spiritual covering and a shelter for her so she can feel safe enough to allow the healing process to happen.

"The best thing you can do is to assure her of your unconditional love by your words and actions," I continued. "She needs your support more than ever. Tell her you are praying for her and will pray *with* her whenever she needs you to do so. Ask *God* to help you understand what she is feeling and how to respond in a positive way. Praying about your response to what she is feeling is as important as praying for God to heal her emotions. And when your wife begins to find wholeness, it's important to cheer her on."

Praying for your wife can help to fine-tune that priceless instrument God has put in your care. And it will ensure that you'll be enjoying some mighty fine music at your house.

SHE SAYS...

Please pray for your wife that:

1. She will enjoy emotional stability.
2. She will have a clear, strong mind.
3. She will not believe lies about herself.
4. She will feel secure in your love.
5. She will have the joy of the Lord.
6. You will be able to understand her feelings.
7. She will live in peace.

HE SAYS...
BY JACK HAYFORD

Pastor Jack is the founding pastor of The Church On The Way and chancellor of The King's College and Seminary in Los Angeles, California. He and his wife, Anna, have been married for 47 years, and they have four grown children and eleven grandchildren.

I've been asked how I, as a praying husband, have prayed for my dear wife, Anna, and upon reflection I realize something of a peculiarity. It's that the starting place for my most significant times of prayer for her has been to pray for myself:

- . . . to pray that I might perceive her task as she sees it, in order to appropriately stand with her as a support—someone who understands the emotions she is feeling and the nature of the challenge as she senses it from her viewpoint.

- . . . to pray that I may be patient and gracious, "feeling with her," the same way Jesus is "touched with the feeling" of my weakness (Hebrews 4:15).

More and more throughout the years of our marriage, the Holy Spirit has helped me to recognize that to love my wife as Christ loves the church (Ephesians 5:25) is to gain a Christlike sensitivity to how she feels. So as I have prayed for her day in and day out for the more than four decades of our marriage, I have found that my greatest effectiveness is in learning to let the Spirit of God sensitize my heart to Anna's present moment—her tasks, her weariness, her joys, her trials, her uncertainties, or her needs.

This kind of praying requires one other thing: a constant clarity of soul in my own heart toward her. Irrespective of any stress-prompted irritations caused by our busy life, notwithstanding any impatience I, in my male-style responses, may have with her female-style actions or responses, I cannot allow my soul to become cluttered with any attitude that will cripple my capacity to pray with an understanding of her heart, patience with her trial, or sensitivity to her perspective.

It's been a slow-grow proposition for me, but according to her loving assessment of my effort, I've grown a whole lot! My conclusion on this is that it is just another case of the effectiveness of *her* prayers for *me!*

Prayer Power

Lord, I am so grateful that You have made (<u>wife's name</u>) to be a woman of deep thoughts and feelings. I know that You have intended this for good, but I also know that the enemy of her soul will try to use it for evil. Help me to discern when he is doing that and enable me to pray accordingly.

Thank You that You have given (<u>wife's name</u>) a sound mind (2 Timothy 1:7). Protect her from the author of lies and help her to cast down "every high thing that exalts itself against the knowledge of God, bringing every thought into captivity to the obedience of Christ" (2 Corinthians 10:5). Give her discernment about what she receives into her mind. I pray she will quickly identify lies about herself, her life, or her future. Help her to recognize when there is a battle going on in her mind and to be aware of the enemy's tactics. Remind her to stick to Your battle plan and rely on the sword of the Spirit, which is Your Word (Ephesians 6:17). May she turn to You rather than give place to negative, upsetting, evil, or disturbing thoughts.

Keep me aware of when my wife is struggling so I can talk openly with her about what is on her mind and in her heart. Enable us to communicate clearly so that we don't allow the enemy to enter in with confusion or misinterpretation. Help me not to react inappropriately or withdraw from my wife emotionally when I don't understand her. Give me patience and sensitivity, and may prayer be my *first* reaction to her emotions and not a last resort.

Although I'm aware that I cannot meet my wife's every emotional need, I know that *You* can. I am not trying to absolve myself from meeting any of her needs, but I know that some of them are intended to be met only by You. I pray that when certain negative emotions threaten her happiness, You will be the first one she runs to, because only You can deliver her from them. Help her to hide herself in "the secret place of Your presence" (Psalm 31:20).

Lord, I pray that You would restore her soul (Psalm 23:3), heal her brokenheartedness, and bind up her wounds (Psalm 147:3). Make her to be secure in Your love and mine. Take away all fear, doubt, and discouragement, and give her clarity, joy, and peace.

Power Tools

Keep your heart with all diligence, for out of it spring the issues of life.

Proverbs 4:23

The Lord redeems the soul of His servants, and none of those who trust in Him shall be condemned.

Psalm 34:22

Do not be conformed to this world, but be transformed by the renewing of your mind, that you may prove what is that good and acceptable and perfect will of God.

Romans 12:2

To be carnally minded is death, but to be spiritually minded is life and peace.

Romans 8:6

By your patience possess your souls.

Luke 21:19

CHAPTER FOUR

HER MOTHERHOOD

A man's work is clear-cut. He knows when it begins and he knows when it ends. He understands when he is successful at what he does and when he is not. And he knows from his paycheck what his value in the marketplace is. A woman whose main occupation is being a mother doesn't know any of these things. She labors for long hours day and night because the work is never done. There are no sick days off, and there's no place to go if she wants to resign. She finds herself in a highly skilled profession, yet she is given only on-the-job training. She often can't see the fruits of her labor, and she won't *really* know whether she's a success for about 25 years after the job begins. And the pay is quite nebulous, if not nonexistent, even though the benefits are great.

In my survey of wives, women voted motherhood as one of their top three needs for prayer, just under prayer for their spirits and for their emotions. They said that one of the most worrisome aspects of parenting is finding the successful balance between being a good mother and being a good wife. Every mother struggles with that balance daily, and whether she says it or not, she often feels guilty about neglecting her husband or her children. And it is not even an issue of equal time, because there is no way that a self-sufficient husband is going to get equal time with a child who can't do anything for himself. She realizes that her husband can dress and feed himself, get himself off to work, and make wise choices on his own. But her children need her for everything, and the younger they are the more they need her. And, opposite of most other jobs, she cannot successfully delegate much of it to someone else.

Your wife needs your prayers to help her find that balance. When she does, it will not only be better for her, but it will bless you *and* your children in countless ways. Your prayers will also help lift the heavy burden of raising the children off your wife's shoulders before this monumental job becomes wearisome and overwhelming. Most importantly, God will work through your prayers to give her peace in the process. And she must find His peace within herself while she is raising her children, because if she doesn't, she won't survive when they grow up and leave home. Your prayers for her as a mother can make the difference in whether her responsibilities become a daily grind of dirty work or a life-giving labor of love.

THE PAIN OF EMPTY ARMS

In every woman there is a longing to do what she was created to do. One of the things a woman's body was created to do is give birth. Her arms were made to hold a child, and she can feel empty when she is denied that privilege for too long. Even women who for one reason or another have *chosen* not to have children still experience pangs of desire to hold a child in their arms from time to time. For women who very much *want* their own children and have been denied that experience, there is a pain so deep that only God can touch it and soothe it. The "barren womb" is never satisfied (Proverbs 30:15,16).

If your wife is not a mother and wants to be, pray that she will find comfort for that ache, even if she no longer mentions it. If you have decided together to not have children and you are certain it is God's will, there may not be any problem. But if one of you wants a child and the other doesn't, this can lead to frustration, resentment, and unfulfillment that can strain the marriage to the point of breaking. It will never be God's will for the two of you to be in disagreement about this. If you are, seek the Lord wholeheartedly together and pray that the two of you will agree in accordance with God's will.

Surprisingly, healing for infertility was mentioned as one of the top needs for prayer for mothers in my survey of women. So pray that God will do whatever necessary in either you or your wife so that this issue will be completely resolved. And don't give up. I've known many people who have been childless, praying for years for a baby, and who then have seen God answer those prayers in one miraculous way or another. This could not have happened without the long-term fervent prayers of husbands and wives seeking a miracle from God. *Often the greatest miracles happen to those who are desperate for one.*

THE WORKING MOM

Children are a guilt trip anyway ("Have I done enough?" "Did I do too much?"), but if your wife is a mother who works *outside* the home, she has to deal with guilt on an hour-by-hour basis. From the time her children are born or come into her life, a part of *her* is always with *them*. This becomes especially painful when there are long periods of time when *they* are not with *her*. Not being there to greet the children when they come home from school, not seeing them learn something new, not being able to take time off from work when a child is sick, missing special events, performances, games, or field trips, wondering if the person caring for the child is doing a good job while knowing that no one could better care for the child than herself—all these contribute to a mother's pain and guilt.

No matter how good or devoted a mother she is, or how great her parenting skills are, every woman wants prayer that she will be a better mom. Working moms are desperate for those prayers because they have to do more with less time. If your wife is a working mom, pray for the time she has with the children to be maximized. Ask God to provide a way for her to not have to work so much, or maybe not at all. Pray for her to be free from the paralyzing burden of condemnation.

DADS HAVE GUILT TOO

Every man I know wants to be more involved in his children's lives and suffers with guilt when his work occupies too much of his time. Of course, it's important for a man to work and support his family. In fact, it's admirable. Men are often not applauded enough for all they do to provide a secure and safe place for their families. There is great pressure on men to be and do everything successfully, and there is a deep sense of failure when they don't feel they are living up to their own or others' expectations of them. That's one of the reasons I wrote *The Power of a Praying Wife*. I know men need the support of their wives' prayers.

With all that said, I want to encourage you as a father to know that your presence in the home is vitally important. It's more important than you probably realize. When you are at home, it gives your wife and children a sense of security, strength, and love. And in addition to that, if you spend a few minutes of undivided attention a day with your children, looking each of them in the eye and talking to them about their lives in an encouraging way, it enables them to believe they are valuable. You have no idea how important your approval is to your family.

There is a way you can be more involved in your children's lives each day while still providing for their needs in the manner you would like. You can *pray* for them. This does not replace your *time* with them, of course. Kids need *you* more than anything. And they need you to pray *with* them. But when you have to be away from them, tell each of your children that you're going to be praying for them while you're gone, and ask them how they specifically want you to pray. Then pray for them periodically during the day, and they will feel your presence and the presence of God. It's a powerful dynamic.

It's also good to pray for your children together with your wife. "If two of you agree on earth concerning anything they ask, it will be done for them by my Father in heaven" (Matthew 18:19). If one can put a thousand to flight, but two can put *ten* thousand to flight (Deuteronomy 32:30), then praying for your children with your wife is powerful. Ask your wife for any insight she has into each child. She sees so much that you may not have time to notice. She knows their struggles, weaknesses, and strengths, and she wants you to know them too. It will give your wife the greatest peace, confidence, and joy to know you are praying.

No matter how much you are paid in a lifetime for the work you do, the time you spend praying for your wife and children is worth far more. In fact, it's priceless. Whenever you pray for them, you are investing in your future together and storing up treasures in heaven. As far as the worth of your *wife's* work as a mother to your children, let me just quote you some lyrics from a song my husband once wrote with Donna Summer. "She works hard for the money, so you better treat her right." Pray, pray, pray!

SHE SAYS...

Please pray for your wife that:

1. She will be guided by God in raising her children.
2. She will have patience with each child.
3. She will have wisdom when disciplining her children.
4. She will teach her children well about the Lord.
5. She will know how to pray for each child.
6. Her children will be obedient and respectful to her.
7. Her children will rise up and call her blessed.

HE SAYS...
BY STEVEN CURTIS CHAPMAN

Steven is a singer and songwriter. He and his wife, Mary Beth, have been married for 16 years, and they have four children.

Though there have been many instances of the powerful effects of prayer in my relationship with my wife, probably one of the most profound experiences came within the last couple of years. Our daughter Emily, who was 13 at the time, began to talk to us about adopting a little sister. Of course, we explained that in order for her to adopt a little sister, we as her parents would have to adopt another daughter. While we have had a great love for the adoption process since we had experienced it through playing a supporting role for some of our closest friends who had adopted several children, my wife was fairly convinced that ours was to remain strictly a supportive role. I, on the other hand, had always been quietly drawn to the idea of sharing the love of our family with a little one who desperately needed just that...the love of a family. I had often come across the scripture in James 1 that talks about looking after orphans and widows and had wondered what the implications of that should be in my own life.

In the spring of 1999, I was asked to sing at a fund-raising event for an adoption agency that we had been supporting for a couple of years. Emily attended with me that night because Mary Beth had to run taxi service for our boys. That night Emily came home with every piece of informative literature on the subject of adoption she could get her hands on, along with the announcement that there was a great need in China for adoptive families. Mary Beth had made a prior agreement to read anything Emily brought home to her but made it very clear that this was not something she was feeling at all inclined to pursue. And with that, the prayers began. Actually, they had been going on for some time, but they definitely intensified on the part of Emily and me. I had a very strong sense that, though this was something I could get very excited about and could push for, it was going to require God's work in Mary Beth's heart to bring her to a place of peace and even desire for this.

Mary Beth's greatest concern was about love and compassion. She feared that she wouldn't be able to love an adopted child as well as she loved our three birth children. How would she deal with that potential discrepancy, and would it even be fair to bring a child into that enviroment? She would say, "I can hardly change the diaper of one of my own nephews sometimes. It's so different with your own child. What if I feel that way, and it is my own child?" Even as we began to move into the process of filling out papers and walking in the direction of adoption, she would lie in bed and cry many nights, saying she just didn't know if she could really do this. So I prayed, and we prayed.

My prayer usually went something like this: "Okay, Father, You know we've done some pretty crazy things before and this may just be the craziest of all. This seems like something You keep placing in our path and I don't want to miss what You have in Your perfect plan for us. But if this really is Your will for us, then You will have to reveal that to Mary Beth and give her faith to believe it for herself. I don't think I'm supposed to force the issue or even strongly encourage this. She knows where I stand and I'm leaving the rest up to You. If this is not for us to do, then that's okay too. Please have Your way and do the work that only You can do."

And work He did. Some day we'll write the book and tell the whole story, but for now, let me jump way ahead and say that on March 16, 2001, Emily, Caleb, Will Franklin, and I got to see a real-life miracle take place right before our eyes. A precious little bundle of life named Shaohannah was placed in Mary Beth's arms for the first time—and there was no shadow of doubt in her eyes that this was *her* daughter. In fact, I am sure that at that very moment Mary Beth would have just as quickly laid her life down for Shaohannah as for any of our other children. Now, Mary Beth will be the first to tell you she has had a hard time believing those words of doubt ever came from her lips. Yes, God did the thing that only He could do, and we are so grateful that He did. And you know what else? The diapers are nothin'!

PRAYER POWER

Lord, I pray that You will help (<u>wife's name</u>) to be the best mother to our children (child) that she can be. Give her strength, and help her to understand that she can do all things through Christ who strengthens her (Philippians 4:13). Give her patience, kindness, gentleness, and discernment. Guard her tongue so that the words she speaks will build up and not tear down, will bring life and not destruction. Guide her as she makes decisions regarding each child. By the authority You have given me, as a believer as well as a husband and father, I break any rebellion or area of disobedience that would erect a stronghold in our children (child) (Luke 10:19). Specifically I lift up (<u>child's name</u>). I bring before You my concern about (<u>name any area of concern that you have for that child</u>).

Lord, I know we cannot successfully raise our children without You. So I ask that You would take the burden of raising them from our shoulders and partner with us to bring them up. Give my wife and me patience, strength, and wisdom to train, teach, discipline, and care for each child. Help us to understand each child's needs and know how to meet them. Give us discernment about what we allow into the home through TV, books, movies, video games, magazines, and computer activities. Give us revelation and the ability to see what we need to see. Show us Your perspective on each child's uniqueness and potential for greatness. Give us a balance between being overprotective and allowing our children to experience life too early.

If we, being evil, know how to give good gifts to our children, how much more will You, our heavenly Father, give good things to us when we ask it of You (Matthew 7:11). So I ask You for the gifts of intelligence, strength, talent, wisdom, and godliness to be in our children. Keep them safe from any accident, disease, or evil influence. May no plan of the enemy succeed in their lives. Help us to raise our children (child) to be obedient and respectful to both of us and to have a heart to follow You and Your Word. I pray that my wife will find fulfillment, contentment, and joy as a mother, while never losing sight of who she is in You.

POWER TOOLS

HER CHILDREN RISE UP AND CALL HER BLESSED; HER HUSBAND ALSO, AND HE PRAISES HER.

PROVERBS 31:28

BEHOLD, CHILDREN ARE A HERITAGE FROM THE LORD, THE FRUIT OF THE WOMB IS A REWARD.

PSALM 127:3

THEY SHALL NOT LABOR IN VAIN, NOR BRING FORTH CHILDREN FOR TROUBLE; FOR THEY SHALL BE THE DESCENDANTS OF THE BLESSED OF THE LORD, AND THEIR OFFSPRING WITH THEM.

ISAIAH 65:23

POUR OUT YOUR HEART LIKE WATER BEFORE THE FACE OF THE LORD. LIFT YOUR HANDS TOWARD HIM FOR THE LIFE OF YOUR YOUNG CHILDREN.

LAMENTATIONS 2:19

FOR THIS CHILD I PRAYED, AND THE LORD HAS GRANTED ME MY PETITION WHICH I ASKED OF HIM.

1 SAMUEL 1:27

CHAPTER FIVE

HER MOODS

I know what you're thinking. You're wondering why I didn't include "Her Moods" in the chapter on "Her Emotions." The reason for this is that the chapter on emotions is very concrete. Solid, identifiable emotions have names like depression, sadness, anxiety, or anger. Moods, as I am referring to them here, are far more difficult to pin down. They are often very hard to recognize, identify, or understand. They can, in fact, seem so nebulous, unexpected, unwarranted, or irrational that many a husband has been reluctant to venture into this unfathomable territory to try and comprehend their cause. But I would like to attempt an explanation of a woman's moods that may help you gain understanding and—who knows—might even make *sense* to you.

First of all, you must keep in mind that there is a process always going on in a woman's mind and soul, unbeknownst to her unsuspecting husband—and perhaps all others in the vicinity. What is happening is that all her thoughts, fears, hormones, responsibilities, memories of previous offenses, the amount of sleep she got last night, the devil's plans for her life, her entire past, and how her hair is behaving that day, are simultaneously competing for her attention. When all these things converge at one moment in time, it can be unbearable. It doesn't matter what might have been happening just a few moments ago, or the last time you talked to her. That was *then*. This is happening *now*. You may find yourself completely taken by surprise because you were not privy to the process. But don't feel bad about that, because even your wife herself may not have recognized it.

Try to understand that as a man you have simple, clearly defined needs, such as food, sex, success, appreciation, and recreation. Your wife, on the other hand, is a complex being. Her needs are so intricate that even she is at a loss for words to explain them to you. Only God, her Creator, can fathom it all.

Her cycle of hormones alone is beyond comprehension. A woman can be emotionally sensitive in the days before, during, and after her monthly cycle. That leaves about three days in the middle when she is normal, and on one of those days she is ovulating, so it's up for grabs how she is going to be that day. So I figure a guy has two good days when it's safe. In addition to that, if there is any stress in her life, if her husband is too busy for her, if she is over 30 and feels like life is passing her by before she ever gets to realize her dream, if her kids are small and need her every second, if her kids are grown and don't need her like they used to, if she is creative and has no way to express it at the moment, if she has gained weight, or if the devil is telling her she has no purpose, then the atmosphere in and around her can be charged with overwhelming frustration. It seems impossible to cope with it all.

If you ever find this phenomenon occurring in your wife, it's best not to say, "What in the world is the matter with you *now?*"

It's better to first pray, "Lord, reveal to me what is happening in my wife and show me what I can do about it."

Then say to your wife, "Tell me what's going on in that pretty head of yours."

She may not be able to articulate an answer that is remotely understandable to you, but the important thing is that she sees you are listening. If she tells you how horrible she thinks she is and she doesn't know what you see in her, don't agree with her. If she says she hasn't forgotten how you have let her down, don't deny it. If she shares with you that she feels like running away or murdering someone, put your arm around her and say, "How can I help you find a more suitable option?"

Then do everything in your power to keep your eyes from glazing over. Don't glance at your watch or the TV remote. Don't allow your head to turn back in the direction of the newspaper or whatever project you are working on at the moment. And above all, keep your mind from thinking about the *more important* things you could be doing. Women have a special ability to spot that from 50 yards away.

Here is some advice that can help you navigate these waters successfully, including a few good lines that always work. Say them to your wife in any order, and then pray for her.

1. "I love you."

2. "You are the greatest woman in the world to me."

3. "You're beautiful when you're moody." (Maybe you shouldn't use the word "moody." "Upset" might be a better choice.)

4. "Tell me what's on your mind, and I promise not to get mad."

5. "How have I let you down?"

6. "How can I make it up to you?"

7. "Have you been getting enough sleep?"

8. "What would make you happy right now?"

9. "I don't have all the answers. But God does."

10. "Do you want to pray about this together?"

This whole process, prayer included, could take less than 15 minutes of your undivided attention, and it will dissipate the power of all those converging forces. What a small investment of time in order to have such great rewards!

Whatever you do, don't ask your wife, "Is it that time of the month again?" She doesn't want her suffering to be dismissed or explained away so easily. Even if that has everything to do with it, she is not able to see that now. And it will do no good to try to force the issue.

In the midst of the complex manifestations of your wife's moods, there will come forth a simple message. It may be a cry for intimacy. It could be a desire to be known and appreciated. Perhaps it is a deep longing for reassurance that everything is going to be okay. Ask God to help you hear the message and show you how to pray accordingly.

SHE SAYS...

Please pray for your wife that:

1. She will have the peace of God.
2. She will not be subject to mood swings.
3. Her hormone levels will be balanced.
4. She will express her feelings openly to you.
5. She will believe that you love her.
6. You will listen and hear what she is saying.
7. She will rely on the Lord more.

HE SAYS...
BY MICHAEL HARRITON

Michael is a music composer. He and his wife, Terry, have been married for 23 years, and they have three grown children.

Men, when your wife screams "Don't touch me!" at the top of her lungs and then crawls into bed and turns off the lights at 7 P.M., it really means, "Don't leave me. Come and get me. Save me. Help!" If she withdraws her hand when you reach out to touch it, that means, "Please keep trying. This is working. Follow the trail of depression and bad vibes. Find me and rescue me."

My beautiful and talented wife picks up after me, does her studio singing, teaches voice lessons, runs my errands, cooks healthy gourmet meals, keeps a spotless house, does laundry, entertains my clients, serves at church, and still manages to sparkle as my dream date! But some days it doesn't take much to send her into an emotional tailspin. It's usually my fault. I'll do something like getting upset at her because my favorite sock has suddenly become an orphan in its drawer.

On those days my wife has thoughts of running away from home, joining the circus or the space program, or buying a one-way ticket to some remote island. She tells me so. One day in particular I reached out to her, and she recoiled as though I were contagious. I tried again, with only slightly better results. (Do women go to school somewhere to learn this stuff?) Finally she said, "I am NOT pretty. I am NOT talented. I am NOT good at anything, nobody wants me, and there is NO PLACE for me ANYWHERE! I am such a disappointment. Such a failure. What do you see in me?"

Guys, when you hear those tough questions, struggle hard for a positive comeback. She may just be testing you. Pass the test with flying colors by reciting a long list of her good qualities and then praying for her. When I remember to do that, along with any necessary apology, it always works.

PRAYER POWER

Lord, I pray for (<u>wife's name</u>) and ask that You would calm her spirit, soothe her soul, and give her peace today. Drown out the voice of the enemy, who seeks to entrap her with lies. Help her to take every thought captive so she is not led astray (2 Corinthians 10:5). Where there is error in her thinking, I pray You would reveal it to her and set her back on course. Help her to hear Your voice only. Fill her afresh with Your Holy Spirit and wash away anything in her that is not of You.

Balance her body perfectly so that she is not carried up and down like a roller coaster. Give her inner tranquility that prevails no matter what is going on around her. Enable her to see things from Your perspective so that she can fully appreciate all the good that is in her life. Keep her from being blinded by fears and doubts. Show her the bigger picture, and teach her to distinguish the valuable from the unimportant. Help her to recognize the answers to her own prayers. Show me how to convince her that I love her, and help me to be able to demonstrate it in ways she can perceive.

Lord, I know that You have "called us to peace" (1 Corinthians 7:15). Help us both to hear that call and live in the peace that passes all understanding. I say to my wife, "Let the peace of God rule" in your heart, and "be thankful" (Colossians 3:15).

POWER TOOLS

THUS SAYS THE LORD: "BEHOLD, I WILL EXTEND PEACE TO HER LIKE A RIVER."

ISAIAH 66:12

SURELY I HAVE CALMED AND QUIETED MY SOUL.

PSALM 131:2

PURSUE RIGHTEOUSNESS, FAITH, LOVE, PEACE WITH THOSE WHO CALL ON THE LORD OUT OF A PURE HEART.

2 TIMOTHY 2:22

WEEPING MAY ENDURE FOR A NIGHT, BUT JOY COMES IN THE MORNING.

PSALM 30:5

THE PEACE OF GOD, WHICH SURPASSES ALL UNDERSTANDING, WILL GUARD YOUR HEARTS AND MINDS THROUGH CHRIST JESUS.

PHILIPPIANS 4:7

CHAPTER SIX

HER MARRIAGE

I lived on a farm and cattle ranch until I was eight years old. We raised *all* our own food. The winter before I turned nine, a severe blizzard killed our cattle. The following spring, hail killed all our crops. We were completely wiped out. By the time summer came, my dad had decided that farming and raising cattle was too hard, and so we moved to the city and what promised to be an easier life.

One of the main things I learned from life on the farm was how carefully you must plant and tend a garden when you know that your life depends on what it produces. If you don't reap a successful crop, there won't be food to eat.

I learned that if you want anything to grow in your garden, you have to start with the right soil. Just as you cannot build a house without a foundation, you can't have a productive, life-giving garden without good, rich soil. Next, you must have the right seeds. What grows in your garden depends on the seeds you plant, so you need to plant what you want to see come up in the harvest. Once you get the garden planted, you have to carefully water the seeds, diligently pull out the weeds around the sprouts that appear, and be on the lookout for pests, bad weather, and other conditions that can destroy it.

Your marriage is like a garden. The soil is enriched and prepared through prayer. Then you have to plant the right kind of seeds—the good seeds of love, fidelity, respect, time, and communication.

SEEDS OF LOVE

Seeds of love are some of the easiest seeds to plant, and their growth is so rapid that you can sometimes see results instantaneously. If seeds of love are planted by our marriage partner, then hope, peace, and happiness will grow in us. These things will give us courage to face our fears, failures, and inabilities. They will give us strength to stand up and resist the things that oppose us.

Of course, you do have to pull out anything growing in the garden that shouldn't be there. Weeding is not the fun part of gardening, but it is one of those necessary chores that must be done. If weeds of hurt, strife, misunderstanding, criticism, selfishness, and anger are allowed to flourish in the marriage garden without being uprooted, they will choke out anything good that is planted. If seeds of lovelessness are planted, we wither and slowly die from the inside out. Sometimes a garden can still look like a garden, but the plants are dead on the inside. They just haven't fallen over yet. Marriages can get that way too. They look fine on the outside, but within, they are dead. This does not fulfill God's plan for our lives, and it certainly doesn't glorify Him.

If you and your wife do not produce enough love to allow each of you to grow into all God created you to be, then your relationship needs to be examined for selfishness, fear, pride, control, or whatever other weed of the flesh is stifling it. If you have serious problems in your marriage, know that

God can work miracles when you pray. He can change hearts and perspectives in an instant. He can uproot seeds of sin, resurrect love where it has died, and make it not only grow again, but flourish.

The Bible says, "Let love be without hypocrisy. Abhor what is evil. Cling to what is good" (Romans 12:9). Cling to what is good in your marriage with all sincerity of heart. Despise what the devil is trying to plant there. Pray that God will show you how to plant *new* seeds of unconditional love. (A garden has to be replanted every year.) With proper care, those seeds of love will produce a great harvest.

SEEDS OF FIDELITY

In order for a garden to not become a salad bar for hungry animals, it needs a fence around it to keep them out. In the same way, the boundaries of marriage are set up for its protection. If we don't watch over the boundaries, something is sure to be stolen from us. Too often people carelessly plant seeds outside the boundaries, and what grows up attracts the attention of creatures that come to devour. They wait outside the garden, and if the fence falls into disrepair because it isn't maintained, they find a way in through the weakest part. When we plant seeds of infidelity, we break down the boundaries and invite unwanted creatures of prey to come in.

A dear Christian friend of mine had a husband who sowed seeds of infidelity outside the garden of his marriage. This attracted a creature of prey who was hungry to take over the garden for herself. That man and this creature scattered their seeds in fields that were not their own, seeds of weeds and briars from which nothing good could ever grow. This eventually destroyed not only one but two marriage gardens, and it was never possible to regain what was lost.

Everyone gets tempted to sow outside his own garden. The ones who resist, and instead deliberately plant seeds of fidelity, reap a harvest of plenty. Even if you have the most perfect marriage ever known to man, the enemy will still try to tear down the fence and destroy it by one means or another. The devil will always look for ways to set a snare for one of you. So your marriage soil is never too good to be beyond the need for enriching prayer. If we think our marriage is so strong that we don't ever need to pray about it, we are deceived. "Therefore let him who thinks he stands take heed lest he fall" (1 Corinthians 10:12).

Pray that God will keep you and your wife from planting anything you will live to regret. Ask Him to show you how to plant seeds of fidelity and build a fence so solid it will be the envy of all your neighbors.

SEEDS OF RESPECT

One of the main reasons marriages fail is that the husband or wife does not seek the other's best interest. The Bible says, "Let no one seek his own, but each one the other's well-being" (1 Corinthians 10:24). When we sow seeds of disrespect in a marriage, we are not seeking the other's well-being, and we will reap a crop of bitterness and strife. Putting our mate's well-being before our own is not only very difficult, it's simply impossible to do on a consistent basis without the Holy Spirit enabling us. That's why we must pray about it.

Because you are a dear brother in the Lord, I want to share something with you that women don't always verbalize to their husbands. This is, your wife does not want to be your mother, nor does she want to be your maid. The former will cause *her* to lose respect for *you;* the latter will make her feel that *you've* lost respect for *her*. I know there are countless things your wife will do that a mother or maid would do also. But if that expectation becomes a way-of-life attitude on your part, she will begin to think of you as a child or as a boss, and it will adversely affect your relationship. The more your wife feels like your mother or your maid, the less she will feel like your lover. Ask God to help you see things from your wife's perspective and show you how to plant seeds of respect in your marriage.

SEEDS OF TIME

You can't have a successful garden if you don't spend enough time in it. It takes many hours to plant, water, feed, nurture, and harvest. In successful marriages the husbands and wives spend time together alone. If your schedules never allow time for you and your wife to be alone with each other, then you are too busy. You need that time of togetherness to talk, to work things out, to share interests and dreams, to just be together in silence, and to have intimate times that are not rushed. I know there are seasons in everyone's life that are especially busy. But when busyness becomes a lifestyle, you've got to consider exactly what it is you're planting. Pray that God will help you plant seeds of time together.

SEEDS OF COMMUNICATION

Words are like seeds. They start out small and grow into something big. If a person plants words of anger, indifference, criticism, impatience, or insensitivity in his marriage, the fruit of those words will be lack of intimacy and warmth, loss of harmony and unity, and the silencing of laughter and joy. These seeds can grow into something big enough to choke out everything else around them.

One of the biggest problems in many marriages is a lack of communication. Wives say, "My husband doesn't really hear what I'm saying. He doesn't listen." Husbands say, "My wife doesn't understand me. She misinterprets things I say." This comes about because men and women think differently. It's one of the ways we complete one another. If a man and a woman inevitably see things from different perspectives, then it stands to reason that they should ask God to help them both see things from *His* perspective. That way they can see them together, from the same viewpoint.

In the garden of a marriage relationship, there will always be a harvest time. "Whatever a man sows, that he will also reap" (Galatians 6:7). If we don't like the crop we're reaping, then it's probably time to plant seeds of a different nature. Seeds are planted through actions, but mostly through words—and when a husband and wife can't communicate well with their words, bad things start growing.

If bad word-seeds have already been planted in your marriage, and fast-growing weeds are choking the life out of your relationship, know that God has given you the tool of prayer to uproot them. Get to the bottom of whatever you see growing out of control, such as bitterness, anger, or unforgiveness, and pray for those things to be dug up and thrown away.

Marriage can seem like heaven. Or it can seem like hell. For most people, it's somewhere in between. That's because it's not easy becoming one with another person, even if that person is the one God created especially for you. There is a lot of growing required. But it's not about causing our mate to grow into *our* image, it's about both husband and wife growing into *God's* image, together.

God can cause a husband and a wife to grow together in a way that makes them more compatible while allowing the two partners to develop their individual gifts and retain their own uniqueness. Marriage does not need to be stifling, forcing two people to lose all individuality. Rather, it can actually provide the perfect environment for the gifts of each person to be developed to the fullest. When the two people in a marriage partnership relate to one another in the way God wants them to, it brings about a fulfilling of each one's purpose that will not happen otherwise. Through prayer, each one can *release* the other rather than control; *encourage* rather than condemn.

God will not bless our disobedience. He doesn't approve when selfishness, deceit, strife, neglect, and cruelty are permitted to grow unchecked in a marriage garden. When we treat our marriage partner in a way that is less than what God wants us to do, not only are we rebelling against the Lord, but we are working against what God wants to accomplish in us as individuals and as a couple.

Ask God to help you and your wife appreciate your differences. Ask Him to show you where you complement each other. Is one of you strong where the other is weak? The very thing that is designed to be our greatest blessing can often become an irritant because we don't ask God to let us see it from *His* perspective. Is there something your wife does or says that bothers you? Tell God about it. He'll show you how to pray.

Divorce doesn't happen because people don't want their marriages to work out. It's usually because the husband or wife believes that things will never change. Ask *God* to change what needs to be changed in either of you. Even if it appears that irreparable damage has already been done in your marriage, that the garden has been hopelessly blighted, know that God can and wants to work a miracle. We have no idea of the wonderful things God has for us when we humble ourselves and love God enough to live His way (1 Corinthians 2:9). This is never more true than in a marriage.

Through prayer you can invite the light of the Lord to bathe and invigorate the garden of your marriage. Then it will bud, blossom, bloom, and grow into a harvest of joy and fulfillment for both of you.

SHE SAYS...

Pray for your marriage that:

1. Love will grow between you and your wife.
2. You and your wife will resist temptation to stray.
3. You will practice mutual respect for one another.
4. The two of you will not live separate lives.
5. You will be friends as well as lovers.
6. You will work together as a team.
7. There will be no divorce in your future.

HE SAYS...
BY MICHAEL OMARTIAN

"A threefold cord is not quickly broken" (Ecclesiastes 4:12). That verse was "manna" to Stormie and me during tough times in our marriage. It seemed that our difficulties often arose out of superficial circumstances, but the enemy of our souls would use anything to destroy the threefold cord that our marriage represented. Confronting, arguing, and trying to reason with each other always came up short. What didn't come up short was praying together. But what a hurdle we had to face just to get to that.

Prayer requires forgetting your own agenda and letting God set the agenda. Many times prayer would focus my attention away from the need to see Stormie change and become more accommodating to me, to instead how *I* could change and be more accommodating to *her*. Scary stuff for the ego! But through prayer we have been able to make changes and work things out. Now we have been married for 28 years and I can't imagine anyone else as my mate. But our problems only work themselves out when she and I join with God to solve them. That threefold cord will not be easily broken.

PRAYER POWER

Lord, I pray that You would establish in me and (<u>wife's name</u>) bonds of love that cannot be broken. Show me how to love my wife in an ever-deepening way that she can clearly perceive. May we have mutual respect and admiration for each other so that we become and remain one another's greatest friend, champion, and unwavering support. Where love has been diminished, lost, destroyed, or buried under hurt and disappointment, put it back in our hearts. Give us strength to hold on to the good in our marriage, even in those times when one of us doesn't *feel* love.

Enable my wife and me to forgive each other quickly and completely. Specifically I lift up to You (<u>name any area where forgiveness is needed</u>). Help us to "be kind to one another, tenderhearted, forgiving," the way You are to us (Ephesians 4:32). Teach us to overlook the faults and weaknesses of the other. Give us a sense of humor, especially as we deal with the hard issues of life.

Unite us in faith, beliefs, standards of morality, and mutual trust. Help us to be of the same mind, to move together in harmony, and to quickly come to mutual agreements about our finances, our children, how we spend our time, and any other decisions that need to be made. Where we are in disagreement and this has caused strife, I pray You would draw us together on the issues. Adjust our perspectives to align with Yours. Make our communication open and honest so that we avoid misunderstandings.

May we have the grace to be tolerant of each other's faults and, at the same time, have the willingness to change. I pray that we will not live two separate lives, but will instead walk together as a team. Remind us to take time for one another so that our marriage will be a source of happiness, peace, and joy for us both.

Lord, I pray that You would protect our marriage from anything that would destroy it. Take out of our lives anyone who would come between us or tempt us. Help us to immediately recognize and resist temptation when it presents itself. I pray that no other relationship either of us have, or have had in the past, will rob us of anything in our relationship now. Sever all unholy ties in both of our lives. May there never be any adultery or divorce in our future to destroy what You, Lord, have put together. Help us to never cast aside the whole relationship just because it has developed a nonworking part. I pray that we will turn to You—the Designer—to fix it and get it operating the way it was intended.

Teach us to seek each other's well-being first, as You have commanded in Your Word (1 Corinthians 10:24). We want to keep You at the center of our marriage and not expect from each other what only *You* can give. Where either of us have unrealistic expectations of the other, open our eyes to see it. May we never waver in our commitment and devotion to You and to one another, so that this marriage will become all You designed it to be.

POWER TOOLS

TWO ARE BETTER THAN ONE, BECAUSE THEY HAVE A GOOD REWARD FOR THEIR LABOR. FOR IF THEY FALL, ONE WILL LIFT UP HIS COMPANION. BUT WOE TO HIM WHO IS ALONE WHEN HE FALLS, FOR HE HAS NO ONE TO HELP HIM UP.

ECCLESIASTES 4:9,10

IF TWO OF YOU AGREE ON EARTH CONCERNING ANYTHING THAT THEY ASK, IT WILL BE DONE FOR THEM BY MY FATHER IN HEAVEN.

MATTHEW 18:19

WHOEVER DIVORCES HIS WIFE AND MARRIES ANOTHER COMMITS ADULTERY AGAINST HER.

MARK 10:11

TAKE HEED TO YOUR SPIRIT, AND LET NONE DEAL TREACHEROUSLY WITH THE WIFE OF HIS YOUTH.

MALACHI 2:15

BE KINDLY AFFECTIONATE TO ONE ANOTHER WITH BROTHERLY LOVE, IN HONOR GIVING PREFERENCE TO ONE ANOTHER.

ROMANS 12:10

CHAPTER SEVEN

HER SUBMISSION

Submit is a verb. *Submitting* is a voluntary action. That means it is something *we ourselves* do. It's not something we make *someone else* do. Just as we can't force another person to love us, we can't force someone to submit to us either. Of course we can *make* that person do what we want. But then that's not true submission.

Submission is a *choice* we make. It's something each one of us must decide to do. And this decision happens first in the heart. If we don't *decide in our hearts* that we are going to willingly submit to whomever it is we need to be submitted to, then we are not truly submitting.

This may be shocking news to you, but an overwhelming majority of wives in my survey said they *want* to submit to their husbands. They *want* their husbands to be the head of the home, and they have no desire to usurp that God-given position of leadership. They know what the Bible says on the subject, and discerning wives want to do what God wants because they understand that God's ways work best.

However, problems often arise in this area because a wife is afraid to submit to her husband for two reasons:

- Reason #1. Her husband thinks submission is only a noun, and he uses it as a weapon.

- Reason #2. Her husband has himself not made the choice in his heart to be fully submitted to God.

Okay, okay! I know that God did not say a wife needs to submit to her husband only if he proves to be worthy. Submission is a matter of trusting in *God* more than trusting in man. But a wife will more easily make the choice to submit to her husband if she knows that he has made the choice to submit to the Lord. It will be a sign to her that it is safe to submit to him. And the goal here is to *help* her, not *force* her, into proper alignment.

Many a wife has a hard time trusting that her husband is hearing from God if he doesn't appear to be submitted to God in the way he treats her. Wives know that after the verse "Wives, submit to your own husbands" (Ephesians 5:22), the Bible says "Husbands, love your wives, just as Christ also loved the church and gave Himself for her" (verse 25). Christ doesn't neglect, ignore, demean, or abuse the church. He doesn't treat her rudely or disrespectfully. He never acts arrogantly or insensitively toward her. Nor does He criticize her and make her feel she is not valuable. Rather He loves her, protects her, provides for her, and cares for her. So while God gives the husband a position of leadership in relationship to his wife, He also requires the price of self-sacrifice from him.

The big question in many women's minds is, "If I submit myself to my husband, will I become a doormat for him to walk on?" The answer to that question depends entirely upon whether her husband believes he should love his wife like Christ loves the church and willingly sacrifices himself for her—or thinks that submission is a noun and that it is something owed him. In other words, does he only consider *his* desires and opinions, to the exclusion of *hers?*

A wife has a hard time giving her husband the reins to her life if she doesn't believe she can trust him to have her best interests at heart as he steers the course of their lives together. She has trouble going along with his decisions when he refuses to consider her thoughts, feelings, and insights on the subject. And if she has submitted to a male in the past and her trust was violated in some way, it is even more difficult for her to trust now.

On the other hand, a woman will do anything for a man who loves her like Christ loves the church. Submission is easy under these conditions. I know a number of women who are married to unbelieving husbands and who have no problem submitting to their husbands, because in each case the husband loves his wife like Christ loves the church, even though he doesn't even know Christ.

Too often people confuse "submit" with "obey." But they are not the same thing. The Bible give commands about obeying other people only in regard to children and slaves, and in the context of the local church. "Children, obey your parents in the Lord, for this is right" (Ephesians 6:1). "Bondservants, be obedient to those who are your masters according to the flesh" (Ephesians 6:5). "Obey those who rule over you, and be submissive, for they watch out for your souls, as those who must give account" (Hebrews 13:17). Since a wife is neither her husband's child nor his servant, and the local church isn't part of a marriage, the word "obey" has no application to the relationship between a husband and a wife.

Submission means "to submit yourself." In light of that, when a husband *demands* submission from his wife, it is no longer true submission. And his demands can become intimidating and oppressive, which breeds resentment. When a husband is more interested in his wife's submission to *him* than he is in his own submission to *God*, then submission becomes a tool to hurt and destroy.

I have seen too many marriages between strong Christian people—high-profile Christian leaders, in fact—end in divorce because the husband *demanded* submission and resorted to verbal or physical abuse in order to get it. My husband has even counseled men like that, men who refused to hear that losing their family was a horrible price to pay for being "right." How much better it would have been for the husband to submit himself to God's hand and then pray for his wife to be able to come into proper order. This kind of situation occurs far too often.

When we submit to God, He doesn't suppress who we are. He frees us to become who we're made to be, within the boundaries of His protection. When a wife submits to her husband, she comes under his covering and protection, and this frees her to become all God created her to be. And trust me, you want that for your wife. Her greatest gifts will prove to be your greatest blessing.

If you feel that your wife is not submissive, pray for her to have a submissive heart, first toward God and then toward you. Then ask God to help you love her the way He does. I guarantee that you will see her submission level rise in direct proportion to the unselfish love you exhibit for her. And let her see that you are seeking God for guidance. If she knows that you are asking God to show you the way, she will follow you anywhere.

SHE SAYS...

Please pray for your wife that:

1. She will understand what submission really is.
2. She will be able to submit in the way God wants her to.
3. You will be completely submitted to God.
4. She will trust God as He works in you.
5. You will take your position as spiritual leader.
6. She will trust you to be the head of the family.
7. Submission will not be a point of contention in your marriage.

HE SAYS...
BY MICHAEL OMARTIAN

I vividly remember, from the time I was a young man, watching my father help my mom with the dishes, throw clothes into the washing machine, make beds, and prepare dinner with my mother. He worked a regular job by day, but he never used that as an excuse for sharply dividing the roles in the family. His actions modeled to me a man who respected, revered, and cherished his wife. He wanted me to know that submission was not a one-sided dynamic, but an action shared equally between two people who both sacrificed for the achievement of one another's goals. I believe that too much has been made of the concept of submission. Where males have taken the heavy-handed approach, it has spawned a woman's movement with justifiable complaints.

Where love, unselfishness, and prayer prevail, the concept of submission is allowed to live and breathe naturally. We men have failed in this area by holding onto notions of some special power we think we have simply because we are men. We are then tempted to lord it over our wives with this power. Yes, God gives us authority, but He also created us equal with our wives and makes us to be one flesh with them. I would be warring with myself if I attempted to gain unbalanced authority over my wife. Again, prayer is the equalizer. I pray for both my wife and myself that we would be in right order toward one another and toward God.

PRAYER POWER

Lord, I submit myself to You this day. Lead me as I lead my family. Help me to make all decisions based on Your revelation and guidance. As I submit my leadership to You, enable (<u>wife's name</u>) to fully trust that You are leading me. Help her to understand the kind of submission You want from her. Help me to understand the kind of submission You want from me. Enable me to be the leader You want me to be.

Where there are issues over which we disagree, help us to settle them in proper order. I pray that I will allow You, Lord, to be so in control of my life that my wife will be able to freely trust Your Holy Spirit working in me. Help me to love her the way You love me, so that I will gain her complete respect and love. Give her a submissive heart and the faith she needs to trust me to be the spiritual leader in our home. At the same time, help us to submit "to one another in the fear of God" (Ephesians 5:21). I know that only You, Lord, can make that perfect balance happen in our lives.

POWER TOOLS

WIVES, SUBMIT TO YOUR OWN HUSBANDS, AS TO THE LORD. FOR THE HUSBAND IS HEAD OF THE WIFE, AS ALSO CHRIST IS HEAD OF THE CHURCH; AND HE IS THE SAVIOR OF THE BODY. THEREFORE, JUST AS THE CHURCH IS SUBJECT TO CHRIST, SO LET THE WIVES BE TO THEIR OWN HUSBANDS IN EVERYTHING. HUSBANDS, LOVE YOUR WIVES, JUST AS CHRIST ALSO LOVED THE CHURCH AND GAVE HIMSELF FOR HER, THAT HE MIGHT SANCTIFY AND CLEANSE HER WITH THE WASHING OF WATER BY THE WORD, THAT HE MIGHT PRESENT HER TO HIMSELF A GLORIOUS CHURCH, NOT HAVING SPOT OR WRINKLE OR ANY SUCH THING, BUT THAT SHE SHOULD BE HOLY AND WITHOUT BLEMISH.

EPHESIANS 5:22-27

HE WHO FINDS HIS LIFE WILL LOSE IT, AND HE WHO LOSES HIS LIFE FOR MY SAKE WILL FIND IT.

MATTHEW 10:39

BE OF THE SAME MIND TOWARD ONE ANOTHER.

ROMANS 12:16

CHAPTER EIGHT

HER RELATIONSHIPS

Awoman needs close friendships with other women. She doesn't need many—it's the quality that counts more than the quantity. But the right caliber of friends is very important.

Your wife doesn't need friends who use her, wear her down, are jealous of her, don't really like her, talk disparagingly about her behind her back, are trying to get close to you, or are so needy and dependent that they are draining. She needs friends who build her up and enrich her life, and allow her to do the same for them. She needs trustworthy and faithful companions to talk to, to pray with, to offer help when she needs it, and with whom she can discuss important topics about which you may not have the slightest interest. She needs friends who will pull for her, contribute to her life, and keep her on the right path, and who always give her a standard to which she can aspire. These kinds of friends will help your wife to grow, and ultimately add to your marriage relationship. Your wife wants you to pray that she will have good, godly friendships.

Relationships with family members are extremely important and must be covered in prayer as well. People are sensitive, and things can get in the midst of *any* relationship and cause it to misfire. But family members in particular have a history of expectations and disappointments, which makes relationships with them very complex.

In-law relationships can be especially delicate. That's why you can't assume that your wife's relationship with your family is going to be fine. In fact, the type of relationship she has with them will depend a lot on you. Your answers to the following questions will reveal how you should be praying.

1. Does your family fully accept your wife, or do they still think that someday you will come to your senses and find the wife of their choice?
2. Do you say good things about your wife to your family members, building her up in their minds?
3. Do you ever complain about your wife in front of your family members or side with them against her?
4. Does your family think of your wife as a blessing, an asset, a valuable person, and a gift from God to you?
5. Is your wife ever viewed by your family as a threat, an endurance test, a mistake, a thorn in their sides, or a cross they have to bear?
6. Does your family welcome your wife with open arms, or do they keep her at arm's length?
7. Has your wife ever indicated to you that her relationship with your family is not what she would like it to be?

Ask God to show you the truth about your wife's relationship with your family. Ask your wife to share her feelings about whether or not she feels accepted by all your family members. Many a wife has suffered in silence for years over not feeling accepted by her in-laws. And many a husband has refused to hear his wife's feelings on the subject because he blamed her for the entire problem.

If your wife reveals something of that nature to you, don't be defensive about it—cover it in prayer. Ask God to show you the truth about the situation. Sometimes it's just that people are different and they don't understand one another. Your wife can't *force* people to love her, yet you might be able to say something to her or your family that would make a difference. But pray about it first. When a husband brings a wife into his family, he owes it to her to pray that she will find favor with each of his family members. Just because *he* fell in love with her doesn't mean *they* will.

Besides good relationships with friends and family members, every married couple needs to have at least two or three other couples with whom they can spend time. It's not always easy to find two people who are married to each other whom you and your wife equally enjoy, so it may require flexibility on someone's part to make it work. But it's worth praying for these couples to come into your lives. If you already have these kinds of friends, pray for the friendships to grow.

The Bible says we should not be "unequally yoked together with unbelievers" (2 Corinthians 6:14). This doesn't mean you can't have any unbelieving friends, but the relationships that influence you the most should be with people who strive to live God's way. We all know unbelievers who make better "Christians" than certain Christians. So pray that God will take out of your lives anyone who will not prove to be a positive influence.

FORGIVENESS IS CRITICAL

Crucial to any relationship is having and maintaining a forgiving heart. It's easy to find something to be unforgiving about, so we have to choose to be a forgiving person. If we don't, our unforgiving heart can overflow at any time into our relationships. For example, have you and your wife ever gone to dinner with other couples and heard a husband or wife make disrespectful, critical, or unflattering remarks about their spouse in front of everyone? It makes everyone at the table feel very uncomfortable. No matter how graciously people might respond, they secretly glance at their watches, design an early escape plan in their minds, and cross that couple off the guest list for their next dinner party. Even if something was said jokingly, everyone there feels the embarrassment or hurt of the person who was ridiculed. The husband or wife may have a legitimate complaint, but will appear like a weakling for dealing with it in such a cowardly way. Everyone knows that the consequences of those words will be evident the next time the offending person wants to be intimate—and the spouse has no interest.

Comments such as these reveal an unforgiving heart on overflow. And an unforgiving person affects everyone around him or her. When husbands and wives are unforgiving toward one another and don't treat each other with respect, not only do *they* suffer, but so do their children, family members, friends, co-workers, and anyone else with whom they come into contact. When a person has unforgiveness in his or her heart toward anyone, people who are around them pick up on it, even if they don't know exactly what it is.

If your wife has any unforgiveness in her heart toward anyone, pray for her to be free of it. If she doesn't get free, it will affect every relationship she has and keep her from becoming all God made her to be.

SHE SAYS...

Please pray for your wife that:

1. She will have close friendships with godly women.
2. She will have good relationships with all family members.
3. She will find favor with her in-laws.
4. She will not be an "injustice collector."
5. She will be able to release hurts from the past.
6. She will forgive others completely.
7. She will experience reconciliation where there is now estrangement.

HE SAYS...
BY KENNETH C. ULMER

Bishop Ulmer is the senior pastor of Faithful Central Bible Church in Inglewood, California. He and his wife, Togetta, have been married for 24 years, and they have 3 children.

The area of prayer that has claimed my most consistent fervent attention is the relationship between my wife and my children. I have been married for almost 25 glorious years, and I have seen the power of God move in our relationship, exemplifying the truth that God is able to do exceedingly abundantly above all that we could ever ask or think. God has especially moved mightily and miraculously in the bond between my wife and my daughters.

My girls were five and three when my wife and I were married. I had been married before, and the prospects for a blended, ready-made family were not good. I saw from the outset that we would need the covering of God on the tender, fragile connection between my old life and the second chance God was graciously giving me. From the very beginning I began to pray against bad stepmother-stepdaughter relationships! And I have seen the Lord form a bond of honesty, understanding, patience, and respect that never could have been created in the natural. Now my daughters are 29 and 27. They and my wife have a real relationship of love and respect. They don't hang out together because they have their own lives, but I have seen God create a closeness that only He could produce.

The Lord has also allowed us to adopt the world's greatest son, who is now 14. He is my beloved son, in whom I am well pleased! I thank God that all of my children are saved and love the Lord. All of us have struggled together, cried together, and prayed together for the protective hand of God on our home and family. We are in many ways the typical pastor's family, but in other ways we are a miracle testimony to the power of God to heal, deliver, and bind together relationships for His glory.

I have also prayed that God would send a few godly women into my wife's life whom she could trust and with whom she could be close. I find that pastors' wives are often the loneliest women because they have no real friends with whom they can be open and honest. They do not know whom they can trust. I prayed for women who would love my wife, pray with her, and stand with her. And I thank God for the friends He has given her with whom she can laugh, cry, and rejoice. I have even found myself thanking God for the friends she can shop with (at least until I get the bills!), knowing that these are times of refreshing fellowship. God has been faithful to answer these prayers.

PRAYER POWER

Lord, I pray for (<u>wife's name</u>) to have good, strong, healthy relationships with godly women. May each of these women add strength to her life and be a strong prayer support for her. Take away any relationship that will not bear good fruit. I also pray for good relationships with all family members. May Your spirit of love and acceptance reign in each one. I pray for a resolution of any uncomfortable in-law relationships for either of us. Show me what I can do or say to make a positive difference. Specifically I pray for my wife's relationship with (<u>name of friend or family member</u>). Bring reconciliation and restoration where that relationship has broken down.

Lord, I pray that (<u>wife's name</u>) will always be a forgiving person. Even if she doesn't feel like it at the moment, help her to forgive out of obedience to You. Show her that forgiveness doesn't make the other person right, it makes *her free*. If she has any unforgiveness that she doesn't realize she has, reveal it to her so that she can confess it before You and be released from it. I especially pray that there would be no unforgiveness between us. Enable us to forgive one another quickly and completely. Help us to remember that You, Lord, are the only One who knows the whole story, so we don't have the right to judge. Make my wife a light to her family, friends, co-workers, and community, and may all her relationships be glorifying to You, Lord.

POWER TOOLS

THE RIGHTEOUS SHOULD CHOOSE HIS FRIENDS CAREFULLY, FOR THE WAY OF THE WICKED LEADS THEM ASTRAY.

PROVERBS 12:26

WHENEVER YOU STAND PRAYING, IF YOU HAVE ANYTHING AGAINST ANYONE, FORGIVE HIM, THAT YOUR FATHER IN HEAVEN MAY ALSO FORGIVE YOU YOUR TRESPASSES.

MARK 11:25

A MAN WHO HAS FRIENDS MUST HIMSELF BE FRIENDLY, BUT THERE IS A FRIEND WHO STICKS CLOSER THAN A BROTHER.

PROVERBS 18:24

LET ALL BITTERNESS, WRATH, ANGER, CLAMOR, AND EVIL SPEAKING BE PUT AWAY FROM YOU, WITH ALL MALICE. AND BE KIND TO ONE ANOTHER, TENDERHEARTED, FORGIVING ONE ANOTHER, JUST AS GOD IN CHRIST FORGAVE YOU.

EPHESIANS 4:31,32

JUDGE NOT, AND YOU SHALL NOT BE JUDGED. CONDEMN NOT, AND YOU SHALL NOT BE CONDEMNED. FORGIVE, AND YOU WILL BE FORGIVEN.

LUKE 6:37

CHAPTER NINE

HER PRIORITIES

Your wife is constantly on trial. Or at least she can often feel that way.

It is the unwritten law of the land that she be judged on how well her children behave, perform, succeed in school, and ultimately turn out in life. She will be silently indicted if she is not active in the church, school, neighborhood, and community. Society holds her responsible for and will pass judgment on how the interior of her house looks, even though there is only hearsay evidence that it always looks that way. (The exterior is blamed on you.)

If she is employed, this further complicates things because there is an unspoken ordinance that says she must serve notice to the rest of her life that her job takes precedence. Above all, she will be held accountable to be a great wife, mother, daughter, friend, and neighbor. And if she fails at even one of the above, she will be put on trial and judged on circumstantial evidence by a not-so-impartial jury. During all the time she spends on any one of these priorities, she worries that she is recklessly endangering the others. She can sometimes feel she has to daily prove her innocence, or else she must plead guilty and suffer the consequences.

It doesn't help matters that she has the prosecutor of her soul forever providing expert witnesses of her failure.

It seems that all of his accusations are sustained, that every one of her objections is overruled. The cross-examination going on in her mind is ruthless. The charges are pressed so hard that they hurt. All infringements of which she stands accused seem too minor to warrant such harsh punishment. She is, after all, only trying to do her best. Why does it never seem to be enough?

Society expects a lot of women. Society expects a lot of men too, but in different ways. Men, for example, have more pressure than women to provide for their families. A woman may *help* provide for her family, but the expectations are not ultimately on her to do it. Even when a woman is the sole provider for her family, if she doesn't make much money or get a great promotion or become successful in her field, no one thinks less of her. A man is not allowed that much slack. But no matter how much a wife contributes to the family income, even if she is the only one working to provide for the family and her husband stays home with the children, she will still be held responsible if her children don't do well socially or academically.

Sometimes your wife may feel the pressure of so many expectations at once that it overwhelms her, and this makes her less effective in getting done what she needs to do. She may even get discouraged and short-circuit. Understanding all this will help you pray for her.

Another one of those great pressures on a woman is that of creating and maintaining a pleasant, inviting, clean, attractive, nurturing, safe haven of a home for the family. A man may be actively involved in making a nice place to live, but he doesn't feel put on trial by it like a woman does. And when a woman feels insecure about her ability to create a comfortable and inviting home, or she has limited time and finances to do it, the home then becomes a source of unending pressure.

For instance, if people walk into Bill and Sara's home and it is messy, unkempt, and unattractive, they don't think Bill is a slob, they think Sara is a bad housekeeper. That's why your wife may be far more upset than you are when family members don't clean up after themselves. Or when you invite someone over to dinner at the last minute without notifying her. She may get irritated about that, not because she doesn't want to see the person, but because when the house is not guest-ready or the dinner is not guest quality, she feels that *she* is the one who will be judged for it. And for many a woman, setting a fine table and serving great food is something that gives her a sense of accomplishment and fulfillment. She is robbed of the chance to do it as well as she knows she can by the element of surprise.

The Bible says it's futile to try to establish a home without asking God to build it. Taking care of a home includes countless small tasks that have to be done again and again, and some tasks are so menial that we don't even think of asking God to be in the midst of them. But He will lighten our load if we yoke up with Him in *all* that we do. Most women have a life outside housekeeping, and they would like to live it. It would take so much of the pressure off of your wife if you would pray that the burden of caring for the home would be lifted. Don't hesitate to ask God what *you* can do to help lighten her load as well. (One of the things I most appreciate about my husband is that he helps around the house.)

Keeping a home can be a very thankless job for a woman, especially if no one is, well, *thanking* her. So remember to show her your appreciation for all she does in the home. She needs to know that you approve, and that you will not thoughtlessly increase her workload.

In setting priorities, a women will generally put everything and everyone before herself. This creates a constant drain on her that may not be noticeable until, one day, she cracks like a bone that has been drained of its calcium. If she is constantly doing for everyone else and never taking time for herself, it will deplete her emotionally and physically. Eventually she will not have anything to give. Pray for her to take time for herself. It will not make her self-centered, it will make her *God-centered*.

It's very difficult for a woman to find the right priorities for her life when so many things are pleading for her attention. Your wife desperately needs your prayers. And if you have been one of those who has passed judgment on her and pronounced sentence, I'm sure you did it with no malice aforethought. Retract your charge, exonerate your wife, and refuse to allow any further miscarriage of justice. Serve notice on the enemy that your wife has been pardoned by the ultimate Judge, the highest legal Authority in the universe, and therefore he has no jurisdiction over her. Her testimony of God's grand acquittal in her life will assure other law-abiding women that they, too, can be free of the rule of high expectations. Then pray that God will reveal to your wife what her priorities should be. As to whether she can actually achieve that perfect balance, the jury is still out.

I rest my case.

SHE SAYS...

Please pray for your wife that:

1. She will remember to put God first.
2. She will take time for you.
3. She will balance her time with the children.
4. She will take needed time for herself.
5. She will be able to create a warm and inviting home.
6. She will always use her time wisely.
7. She will understand what her priorities are.

HE SAYS...
BY MICHAEL OMARTIAN

I know how debilitating life can be when it has no order or priority. Our tasks as men may seem complicated, but I believe they are relatively simple compared to what our wives take on. I spend a lot of my prayer time for Stormie asking God to bring an order to her life so that she may experience joy and peace in the midst of all she has to do. The absence of joy and peace in either one of us directly affects our marriage.

Each of us needs to encourage his wife. "Thank you for doing such a great job," "Thank you for taking good care of the kids," "Thank you for being my wife," are words that cannot be spoken enough. In addition, we must each pray for our wife to seek God and hear from Him what He has given her to do. If we don't pray, we can short-circuit the path and the priorities the Lord has for her. Praying and supporting God's purposes in my wife helps clear a pathway for her to be effective.

I always used to believe that stress was chiefly the domain of us guys. Yeah, right! *I* was sitting in the golf cart, waiting at the eleventh tee, telling my golf partner how happy and relieved I was to be able to take a few hours off to play a round of golf. *Stormie* was in the middle of a book deadline, all the while home-schooling our daughter, taking care of the house, juggling speaking engagements, and taking time for her always-complaining husband.

Our wives probably have more to deal with than we do. Men tend to handle fewer decisions—the larger, more obvious ones. A wife has to make decisions about many details, both small and large. I have asked God to help Stormie set clear priorities so that she isn't drained of life and energy. And God has answered that prayer countless times.

PRAYER POWER

Lord, I lift up (<u>wife's name</u>) to You today and ask that You would be in charge of her life. Show her how to seek You first in all things, and to make time with You her first priority every day. Give her the wisdom to know how to effectively divide up her time, and then to make the best use of it. Show her the way to prioritize her responsibilities and interests and still fulfill each role she has to the fullest. Show her how to find a good balance between being a wife, being a mother, running a home, working at a job, serving in the church and community, and finding time for herself so that she can be rested and refreshed. Release her from the guilt that can weigh her down when these things get out of balance. In the midst of all that, I pray that she will take time for me without feeling she is neglecting other things. Give her the energy and the ability to accomplish all she needs to do, and may she have joy in the process.

Lord, I pray that You would help (<u>wife's name</u>) to make our home a peaceful sanctuary. Regardless of our financial state, give her the wisdom, energy, strength, vision, and clarity of mind to transform our dwelling into a beautiful place of refuge that brings joy to each of us. I ask You to lift from her the burden of caring for our home and give her peace about it. Show me how I can encourage and assist her in that.

Holy Spirit, I invite You to fill our home with Your peace, truth, love, and unity. Keep it safe, and let no one enter our home who is not brought here by You. Through wisdom let our house be built, and by understanding may it be established. By knowledge may the rooms be filled with all precious and pleasant riches (Proverbs 24:3,4). Reveal to us anything that is in our house that is not glorifying to You, Lord. I say that "as for me and my house, we will serve the LORD" (Joshua 24:15).

Give (<u>wife's name</u>) the grace to handle the challenges she faces each day, and the wisdom to not try to do more than she can. Teach her to clearly recognize what her priorities should be, and enable her to balance them well.

POWER TOOLS

TO EVERYTHING THERE IS A SEASON, A TIME FOR EVERY PURPOSE UNDER HEAVEN.

ECCLESIASTES 3:1

SEEK FIRST THE KINGDOM OF GOD AND HIS RIGHTEOUSNESS, AND ALL THESE THINGS SHALL BE ADDED TO YOU.

MATTHEW 6:33

UNLESS THE LORD BUILDS THE HOUSE, THEY LABOR IN VAIN WHO BUILD IT.

PSALM 127:1

SHE WATCHES OVER THE WAYS OF HER HOUSEHOLD, AND DOES NOT EAT THE BREAD OF IDLENESS.

PROVERBS 31:27

THE LAW OF HIS GOD IS IN HIS HEART; NONE OF HIS STEPS SHALL SLIDE.

PSALM 37:31

CHAPTER TEN

HER BEAUTY

I don't care how young or old, perfect or imperfect, confident or fearful, or mature or immature she is, every woman would like to be more beautiful than she is now. And most women don't think they are as beautiful as they really are. I have never met a woman who would not enjoy being told that she is beautiful, especially by the man in her life. If you find a woman who doesn't want to be told she is beautiful, it's probably because she has gone too many years without hearing it, or perhaps when she did hear it she was violated in some way because of it. Whatever the case, she is responding out of hurt.

God made women beautiful. The women of the Bible, such as Sarah, Rachel, Rebekah, and Esther, were exceptionally beautiful, and who can doubt the beauty in Mary and Eve. Inherent in a woman is the desire to see beauty, both in herself and in her surroundings. It is a natural instinct God has put there because He wants her to desire *Him*, the most beautiful of all. He wants her to look to Him so she can reflect *His* beauty (Psalm 27:4).

The main thing that makes a woman beautiful is knowing that she is loved. That's why having God's Spirit living in her and spending time in God's presence in praise and worship is the most effective beauty treatment available. His love beautifies her inside and out.

Her husband's love also makes a woman beautiful. A woman who is not loved will wither and die. One of the reasons raising children can be such a great fulfillment to a woman is that love and affection are flowing through her and to her all day long. But as great as that love is, she needs her husband's love more. His love fulfills her as a person. It makes her rich. It causes her to *feel* beautiful. And all that goodness flows back into his life in return. (My husband has always told me that I am beautiful, even when I was at my worst. Sometimes I tell him I hope he'll never get his vision checked. But I always feel beautiful when he says it.)

Your wife is beautiful. Even though she may not be perfect, there is beauty in her. I know this because you would not have married her if you had't seen her beauty. No man marries a woman if he can't find anything beautiful about her. She has to appeal to him in some way. And no matter how long you are married, you will always be able to find that beauty in your wife if you love her enough to look for it and tell her when you see it. The more a man encourages a woman to feel beautiful, the more beautiful she will become.

Now you may be thinking about that song from *My Fair Lady* called "Why Can't a Woman Be More Like a Man?" In fact, you may even be singing it to yourself at this very moment. But let me remind you that women are *different* than men. There is a popular book out with a title suggesting that men and women come from different planets. I believe that is a serious understatement. Men and women are actually from two different *galaxies*. That's why there is no way a woman can be more like a man and still be a woman. So even though you may not be able to fathom the importance of praying for your wife's beauty, you'll just have to trust me on this one. I know what I'm talking about, so please hear me out. How your wife feels about herself is ultimately as important to *your* happiness as it is to hers.

Although you cannot be responsible for the image of herself that your wife brought into your marriage, you *can* contribute either positively or negatively to the image she grows into. Your words have more power to bring out the beauty in your wife than you ever dreamed possible.

My friend Terry was shopping with her husband one day in a department store and she asked him, "Is there anything you want here?"

Her husband, Michael, turned to her and said, "I don't want anything in this place but you."

Who can doubt that those words made her feel beautiful? Those are the kind of words I'm talking about.

If your wife was devalued and made to feel unattractive by her parents, siblings, or peers when she was young, she may not attribute beauty and worth to herself now. Even though many people may tell her differently, there are only two who can actually make her *believe* she is beautiful—God and you. But even *you* will not be able to convince her if *God* doesn't speak to her first. No matter how much a man tells a woman she is beautiful and valuable, if she doesn't believe it inside herself, it will never be enough. That's where your prayers can make all the difference. Your prayers can set her free from lies of the past and enable her to hear God speak the truth to her heart.

Your prayers will also help your wife find that balance between arrogance and self-flagellation. And every woman must find it in order to have a healthy self-image. No one wants to be around a person who constantly berates herself over how unattractive she is. And no one can tolerate a woman who conceitedly believes she is more beautiful than anyone else.

While most women don't fall into either of those extremes, far too many women do not consider themselves as attractive as they are. That's because women are bombarded with the world's image of what a beautiful woman is supposed to look like. Unless she is a certain size, with certain measurements, with a certain type of hair, eyes, lips, skin, and fingertips, she is made to feel she is not attractive. Pray for your wife to be free from the tyranny of the world's spirit and to get her eyes focused on the beauty of the Lord. His reflection will make her more beautiful than anything else.

A female's need for this kind of affirmation starts early in her life. When my daughter was only two, every Sunday I would get her dressed for church in one of her pretty dresses. I would tell her she looked beautiful, and I could see that it pleased her. But then I always sent her out to the other room to show her dad. If *he* noticed her and told her she looked beautiful, she lit up like a light. No matter what age a woman is, receiving that kind of approval from the man in her life makes her glow. So not only should you tell your wife how beautiful she is, but you should tell your daughter also. She needs that from you more than you will ever know. And while you're at it, tell your mother and your grandmother. It doesn't matter whether a woman in your life is 2 or 102—you have the power to turn on the light.

SHE SAYS...

Please pray for your wife that:

1. She will know that she is loved by God.
2. She will sense the beauty of the Lord in herself.
3. She will feel loved by you.
4. She will value herself.
5. She will find time to take care of herself.
6. She will know how to make herself more attractive.
7. You will always think she is beautiful.

HE SAYS...
BY MICHAEL OMARTIAN

We men have a tendency to discount the importance of our wives' feeling beautiful. Sometimes I wonder why Stormie makes such an effort to keep herself attractive. Make no mistake, I appreciate the results—but the point is that she views her beauty as an integral part of her being, as do most women, so therefore it's important for me to pray that she sense the beauty that God has put in her. In addition to that, my wife never had parents or family members tell her she was beautiful, in fact quite the opposite. So she grew up being convinced that she wasn't attractive.

After a recent emergency surgery, Stormie said to me in a rather discouraged tone, "Michael, today you are seeing me at my worst," to which I responded, "Honey, you see me at my worst every day!" We men have a profound effect on our wives' self-esteem when we build them up and tell them how beautiful they are. In the area of beauty, my prayer for Stormie is that God will reflect His beauty through her. Trust me, it's working!

PRAYER POWER

Lord, I pray that You would give (wife's name) the "incorruptible beauty of a gentle and quiet spirit, which is very precious" in Your sight (1 Peter 3:4). Help her to appreciate the beauty You have put in her. Help me to remember to encourage her and speak words that will make her feel beautiful.

Where anyone in her past has convinced her that she is unattractive and less than who You made her to be, I pray that You would replace those lies with Your truth. Keep any hurtful words that have been spoken to her from playing over and over in her mind. I pray that she will not base her worth on appearance, but on Your Word. Help her to see herself from Your perspective. Convince her of how valuable she is to You, so that I will be better able to convince her of how valuable she is to me.

Show my wife how to take good care of herself. Give her wisdom about the way she dresses and adorns herself so that it always enhances her beauty to the fullest and glorifies You. But remind her that time spent in Your presence is the best beauty treatment of all. Make my wife beautiful in every way, and may everyone else see the beauty of Your image reflected in her.

POWER TOOLS

CHARM IS DECEITFUL AND BEAUTY IS PASSING, BUT A WOMAN WHO FEARS THE LORD, SHE SHALL BE PRAISED.

PROVERBS 31:30

DO NOT LET YOUR ADORNMENT BE MERELY OUTWARD—ARRANGING THE HAIR, WEARING GOLD, OR PUTTING ON FINE APPAREL—RATHER LET IT BE THE HIDDEN PERSON OF THE HEART, WITH THE INCORRUPTIBLE BEAUTY OF A GENTLE AND QUIET SPIRIT, WHICH IS VERY PRECIOUS IN THE SIGHT OF GOD.

1 PETER 3:3,4

THE KING WILL GREATLY DESIRE YOUR BEAUTY; BECAUSE HE IS YOUR LORD, WORSHIP HIM.

PSALM 45:11

GIVE UNTO THE LORD THE GLORY DUE TO HIS NAME; WORSHIP THE LORD IN THE BEAUTY OF HOLINESS.

PSALM 29:2

HE HAS MADE EVERYTHING BEAUTIFUL IN ITS TIME.

ECCLESIASTES 3:11

CHAPTER ELEVEN

HER SEXUALITY

Be honest, now. Did you skip right to this chapter without reading the previous ten? If you did, don't feel bad about it. It's quite understandable and totally natural. Sex is not only a man's strongest drive, but also one of his greatest needs. (You may already know that.) In my book *The Power of a Praying Wife*, I put the things dearest to a man's heart at the beginning. "His Sexuality" is the fourth chapter. (I didn't make it the first chapter because it is, after all, a Christian book.) In the book you're reading now, I have put the greatest concerns of a *woman's* heart in the beginning. That's why "Her Sexuality" falls in about the middle. (Remember, I chose these chapters according to the results of my survey of women.)

There's a reason that sexuality doesn't rank as high on a woman's list as it does on a man's, and I believe it's because sexuality is a *very* complex issue for a woman. It is extremely hard for her to separate herself from emotions, memories, thoughts, and experiences and just be strictly physical. She doesn't seek to gratify only a physical need, there's an emotional one as well.

Your wife's sexuality is wrapped up in two things:

1. How she feels about herself

2. How she feels about you

The way a woman feels about *herself* has a lot to do with how she has been treated by men throughout her life. If she has been abused, ignored, demeaned, disrespected, violated, or simply not valued, she will not value herself. Even if it was not her husband who perpetrated this cruelty, the fact that she endured it will still cause her to have a hard time responding to him. As unfair as that may seem, if a woman doesn't *feel* attractive or sexy, it's difficult for her to act like she is. However, a man can reassure his wife of how attractive she is to him and how much he loves her, and feeling attractive and loved makes a woman want to share herself with her husband in the most intimate ways.

The way your wife feels about *you*—if she is angry, unforgiving, disappointed, wounded, or bitter—will immensely affect her desire for intimacy. If you have hurt her in one way or another, even if it was completely unintentional, it may cause her to withdraw physically in self-protection. It doesn't matter that the wound was inflicted 30 days ago and you haven't even thought about it for the past 29. If it has not been resolved satisfactorily in *her* soul, it will affect your sexual relationship. When she's upset with you, intimacy is the furthest thing from her mind.

For a woman, sex comes out of affection. She has no desire to be affectionate with a man who makes her feel hurt and neglected. Though it's possible for a man to perform sexually without feeling emotionally involved, it's not that way with a woman. She can do it, but it makes her feel like she should be getting paid. A woman's true sexuality is wrapped up in how loved and valued she feels, and it's very difficult for her to give herself to someone who has made her feel bad.

Trust is also a huge factor in a successful sexual relationship. Your wife must be able to trust you. She can tolerate mistakes in other areas if she knows you are truthful. If either of you has violated the other's trust, pray for complete repentance, forgiveness, and healing. A woman never fully gives her body, mind, and emotions to a man she doesn't trust.

If there has been sexual infidelity in your relationship, you need the prayers and support of strong, qualified, trustworthy Christian counselors who believe in the power of God to transform, renew, and bring total restoration. The betrayal must be fully confessed and thoroughly repented of, and forgiveness must be sought. Pray for sexual purity to be restored in the heart of each of you and for fidelity to be an uncompromising way of life. If these things are not the case, all unresolved hurts will be brought to the marriage bed. There has to be complete healing in this area before trust returns, and only God can heal you both and restore that trust.

Many couples have sexual problems in their marriages because one or both of them had improper sexual experiences *before* they were married. If that happened to either of you, pray to have those soul ties broken so you can be set free from their effects. You don't need the ghosts of former relationships brought into the bedroom.

According to the Scriptures, a husband and wife cannot rightfully withhold their bodies from one another. But at the same time, they have to be sensitive to each other's needs and conditions. If one of them is ill or in pain, this should be considered and respected. Often a woman will be too exhausted, but it's nothing personal. There is so much vying for your wife's attention—from raising children and taking care of a home, to work and finances, to emotional stress and hormone ups and downs—and she wants you to be considerate of this. But allowing this part of your life to become neglected is not good either. A woman can get sidetracked by many things and end up neglecting the sexual relationship with her husband. That's why it's important to pray about it.

Sex needs to be a priority in a marriage. Men already know that. Women don't always see it that way. Far too often a wife does not understand how great her husband's need for sex actually is. That's why it's good for you to pray that your wife will gain a clear understanding of this and give you the physical intimacy you need. And you don't have to feel like you're being selfish in doing that. You're not. You are watching over and spiritually covering a vital part of your marriage that, if neglected, could lead to your marriage's destruction. You can't leave this highly important aspect of your relationship up to chance.

I know this may sound strange to you—and don't get mad at me for saying it, because it's what the women in my survey said—but women want to be able to share affection with their husband without always having it lead to the sex act. Your wife wants a sense of togetherness—a hug, a kiss, a simple touch, an embrace—that doesn't always lead to physcial intimacy. Sometimes she needs emotional connection, affirmation, and closeness without having to perform.

There is nothing more attractive to a woman than a man who is strong in the Lord. It makes him irresistible. I have seen unattractive men become quite handsome and appealing when they come to know the Lord, grow in His ways, and become more like Him. If you want to be more attractive to your wife, grow deeper in the Lord. Let God mold your heart, and He will also enhance your appearance as you are transformed into His likeness. There must be 50 ways to *keep* your lover, and this is definitely one of them. And I'm sure, with God's help, you can think of 49 more.

SHE SAYS...

Please pray for your wife that:

1. Your sexual relationship will be fulfilling for both of you.
2. You will be unselfish with one another.
3. Romance will stay alive in your marriage.
4. There will be great affection and desire between you.
5. She will be understanding of your needs.
6. She will not be too exhausted to be intimate.
7. You will be able to please one another sexually.

HE SAYS...
BY MICHAEL OMARTIAN

My wife is a "babe"! She was the first day I met her, and she continues to be so to this very moment. (Let's face it, men, most of us married over our heads.) But Stormie's beauty is not her sole responsibility though, because, believe it or not, *I* have something to do with it. It begins when I vow to revere her in marriage and not violate our sexual trust at any time. I purpose to not allow Satan to destroy our bond. I'm not perfect, and at times I fail in my thoughts, but I do recognize the power of our culture, as orchestrated by the enemy, to make us view our mates as somehow less beautiful and interesting physically, especially after many years of marriage. We're being pushed to fantasize and to dabble in sin. But God will keep us sexually pure if we ask Him. He will keep us away from temptation and infidelity if we seek Him for that.

I pray that our sex life will be beautiful and fulfilling, just as it always has been. No fantasy could ever compete with what God has for us. I also pray for my wife to feel good about who she is. That's very important too.

PRAYER POWER

Lord, I pray that You would bless (<u>wife's name</u>) today, and especially bless our marriage and our sexual relationship. Help me to be unselfish and understanding toward her. Help her to be unselfish and understanding toward me. Teach us to show affection to one another in ways that keep romance and desire alive between us. Where one of us is more affectionate than the other, balance that out. Help us to remember to touch each other in an affectionate way every day. I pray that how often we come together sexually will be agreeable to both of us.

Show me if I ever hurt her, and help me to apologize in a way that will cause her to forgive me completely. Any time we have an argument or a breakdown of communication, enable us to get over it quickly and come back together physically so no room is made for the devil to work. If ever the fire between us dies into a suffocating smoke, I pray that You would clear the air and rekindle the flame.

Help me to always treat my wife with respect and honor and never say anything that would demean her, even in jest. Help me to be considerate of her when she is exhausted or not feeling well. But I also pray that she would understand my sexual needs and be considerate of those as well. Only You can help us find that balance.

Make our sexual relationship fulfilling, enjoyable, freeing, and refreshing for both of us. May our intimacy bond the two of us together and connect our hearts and emotions as well as our bodies. Help us to freely communicate our needs and desires to one another.

Keep our hearts always faithful. Take out of our lives anyone or anything that would cause temptation. Where there has been unfaithfulness in thought or deed on the part of either of us, I pray for full repentance, cleansing, and release from it. Keep us free from anything that would cause us to neglect this vital area of our lives. May our desire always be only for each other. Renew and revitalize our sexual relationship, and make it all You created it to be.

POWER TOOLS

THE WIFE DOES NOT HAVE AUTHORITY OVER HER OWN BODY, BUT THE HUSBAND DOES. AND LIKEWISE THE HUSBAND DOES NOT HAVE AUTHORITY OVER HIS OWN BODY, BUT THE WIFE DOES. DO NOT DEPRIVE ONE ANOTHER EXCEPT WITH CONSENT FOR A TIME, THAT YOU MAY GIVE YOURSELVES TO FASTING AND PRAYER; AND COME TOGETHER AGAIN SO THAT SATAN DOES NOT TEMPT YOU BECAUSE OF YOUR LACK OF SELF-CONTROL.

1 CORINTHIANS 7:4,5

BECAUSE OF SEXUAL IMMORALITY, LET EACH MAN HAVE HIS OWN WIFE, AND LET EACH WOMAN HAVE HER OWN HUSBAND. LET THE HUSBAND RENDER TO HIS WIFE THE AFFECTION DUE HER, AND LIKEWISE ALSO THE WIFE TO HER HUSBAND.

1 CORINTHIANS 7:2,3

MARRIAGE IS HONORABLE AMONG ALL, AND THE BED UNDEFILED.

HEBREWS 13:4

THIS IS THE WILL OF GOD, YOUR SANCTIFICATION: THAT YOU SHOULD ABSTAIN FROM SEXUAL IMMORALITY; THAT EACH OF YOU SHOULD KNOW HOW TO POSSESS HIS OWN VESSEL IN SANCTIFICATION AND HONOR, NOT IN PASSION OF LUST, LIKE THE GENTILES WHO DO NOT KNOW GOD.

1 THESSALONIANS 4:3-5

FLEE SEXUAL IMMORALITY. EVERY SIN THAT A MAN DOES IS OUTSIDE THE BODY, BUT HE WHO COMMITS SEXUAL IMMORALITY SINS AGAINST HIS OWN BODY.

1 CORINTHIANS 6:18

CHAPTER TWELVE

HER FEARS

Anyone who has ever watched the news on TV or read the daily newspaper knows there is plenty to be afraid of in this world. Even the strongest, most godly, faith-filled man or woman has something to fear at one time or another. Women feel especially vulnerable and have their own special set of "what ifs" that have to do with threats to their safety and security and that of their families: "What if someone breaks into the house?" "What if we don't have enough money to pay the mortgage?" "What if my husband dies or is injured?" "What if something bad happens to my children?" "What if I get sick and can't care for my family?" These are very real and legitimate concerns. But when fear about them grips and torments and rules a woman's life, it can become a spirit of fear that is paralyzing.

We can give place to a spirit of fear when we experience something traumatic or frightening. Or when we *witness* something that is. Whether we admit it or not, it causes us to doubt that God is really in control and that He will protect us. When the power and presence of fear outweighs our assurance of the power and presence of God, we can become tormented by a spirit of fear.

The opposite of fear is faith—something we all could use more of in our lives. But getting from fear to faith is a lot harder to do when fear has become a controlling factor. That's why a person who has been overtaken by fear needs prayer. And a husband's prayer for his wife to be set free from fear is powerful. Your prayers for your wife can help her recognize that fear does not come from God (2 Timothy 1:7), and that the perfect love of God removes fear from her soul (1 John 4:18). Your prayers can also help her have faith strong enough to believe that God loves her, is in control of her life, and will not leave or forsake her.

Besides being weighed down by her fear of physical danger and lack of provision for herself and the people she loves, a woman may also suffer from fear of man. There are few women who don't care what anyone thinks about them, their children, their homes, their work, their appearance, their husbands, or their abilities. A certain amount of caring is normal, but when a concern over what other people think adversely affects how a woman behaves, it becomes a fear of man. The fear of man can keep your wife driven to be perfect, or so intimidated that she is afraid to do anything for fear of making a mistake. Your prayers can help your wife to be ruled by the fear of God and not the fear of man.

Even if it doesn't appear to be a full-fledged fear, the thing a woman struggles with most—such as food, weight, relationships, self-worth, appearance, finances, guilt, or self-doubt—usually has its root in the fear of something. The Bible says to "watch and pray, lest you enter into temptation. The spirit indeed is willing, but the flesh is weak" (Matthew 26:41). If your wife has something she considers to be a constant struggle, a weakness of her flesh, or temptation in her life, she needs you to pray with her that God will give her the strength to resist it and be set free.

Do you know what your wife's greatest struggle is? Are you aware of her deepest fears? You may already have a good idea, but if you're not absolutely sure, ask her. Say, "Tell me what you struggle with or fear most in your life, because I want to pray for you about it." You may be completely surprised at her response. Many of us have deep fears that we never share. When I asked my husband that same question years ago, he said he was afraid of not being a good father. I was very surprised to hear that because he had never given any indication it was a particular concern. His fear prompted me to pray specifically for his relationship with his children.

Too often, women carry burdens in their lives that are far heavier than their delicate shoulders were created to bear. Remember, no matter how strong your wife appears to be, she is fragile. Even though a woman may appear strong to the point of hardness, it's usually because she felt she had to be for one reason or another. Ask God to show you whether your wife is carrying something she shouldn't. If so, you can bear part or all of the weight of that thing in prayer.

Another ploy of the enemy of your wife's soul is to put deep discontent in her heart. It's one thing to see where your life needs to improve, and then pray for that and be patient to wait on God for His answer. It's another thing to hate your life. That makes us sick and bitter. Sometimes a woman fears that the difficult spot she's in at the moment is as good as it gets, and that things will never change. That hopeless mindset is torturous for any woman, and I believe it is one of the tactics the enemy uses to create unrest and strife and keep a woman in constant fear. Often women struggle with deeply wanting certain things to happen, yet having to wait such a discouragingly long time for prayers about those things to be answered. Pray that your wife can see her struggles and fears as an opportunity to depend on God in a greater way. Pray that she will be content with her life and be able to trust that God has her where she is for a purpose.

Fear that prompts us to pray is beneficial. Fear that paralyzes and torments us is destructive. Don't allow fear in your wife to keep her from moving into all God has for her.

SHE SAYS...

Please pray for your wife that:

1. She will not be ruled by a spirit of fear.
2. She will submit her struggles to God.
3. She will have no fear of man.
4. She will be able to resist any temptation.
5. She will find her security in the Lord.
6. She will depend on God and not fear the attacks of the enemy.
7. She will have the peace of God.

HE SAYS...
BY JAMES ROBISON

James is an evangelist, the president of Life Outreach International in Fort Worth, Texas, and the co-host of the Life Today *television program. He and his wife, Betty, have been married for 38 years, and they have three children and eleven grandchildren.*

I have been blessed by God with the most wonderful wife. Only God could have designed such a perfect mate, friend, mother, grandmother, and now, miraculously, co-host of the *Life Today* television program.

Betty was plagued with a spirit of fear for much of her life. It manifested itself in feelings of low self-esteem, a horror of failure or disappointment, and an overwhelming desire to perform in some way in order to gain acceptance. But the fear of failing in the attempt to perform caused her emotions and her mind to jam. She used to explain that, even before tests in school, she would experience what she considered serious panic attacks. She felt that she had little to offer others, so she simply dedicated herself to being a devoted wife and a committed mother. She accomplished this worthy mission to great effect, but her feelings of inferiority about sharing with others basically kept her closed off, and kept her mostly to herself as far as the public was concerned.

In my heart, I knew that if the world could see the beauty, spiritual depth, and true wisdom that filled this woman's inner being, she would be an indescribable blessing. I prayed for many years that God would grant her the peace of mind and the confidence to willingly open herself to others so that the river of life which ran so deeply within her could spill over and impact others. As I prayed, I could sense her desire to overcome, and God gave me the insight to constantly encourage her. As I poured on the praise and confidence-building encouragement, it was like watering a beautiful flower.

Every time she would share just a little in a small group, I would point out how mightily others had been blessed. I would keep telling her that the beauty God had placed within her would inspire others to trust Him to enable them to overcome whatever difficulties they faced in life. God answered the prayer, and we saw Him release a life-giving flow that brings admiration and expressions of gratitude from millions of people throughout North America and the mission fields of the world. I sincerely believe, based on the comments of others, that Betty is one of the most loved and respected women alive today. She is living proof of the power of prayer. Because of this miraculous transformation of the life of Betty Robison, millions will live in fullness on this earth and then for all eternity in the presence of our great God and Father!

PRAYER POWER

Lord, I pray that You would help (<u>wife's name</u>) to "be anxious for nothing" (Philippians 4:6). Remind her to bring all her concerns to You in prayer so that Your peace that passes all understanding will permanently reside in her heart. Specifically I pray about (<u>anything that causes your wife to have fear</u>). I ask You to set her free from that fear and comfort her this day.

Teach me to recognize the ploy of the enemy every time he tries to steal life from my wife by bringing fear to torment her. I stand against any enemy attacks targeted at my wife, and I say that a spirit of fear will have no place in her life. Strengthen her faith in You, Lord, to be her Defender.

I pray that (<u>wife's name</u>) will not be tormented by the fear of man. Enable her to rise above the criticism of others and be delivered from fear of their opinions. May her only concern be with pleasing You. I say to my wife, "Be strong in the Lord and in the power of His might" (Ephesians 6:10). "In righteousness you shall be established; you shall be far from oppression, for you shall not fear; and from terror, for it shall not come near you" (Isaiah 54:14). Enable my wife to rise up and say, "The LORD is my light and my salvation; whom shall I fear? The LORD is the strength of my life; of whom shall I be afraid?" (Psalm 27:1).

Lord, give (<u>wife's name</u>) strength to stand strong in the midst of the tough times of her life. Sustain her with Your presence so that nothing will shake her. Enable her to rise above the things that challenge her. Specifically I lift up to You (<u>your</u>

wife's greatest need, weakness, struggle, or tempta-tion). Help her separate herself from that which tempts her. I say to (wife's name) that "no tempta-tion has overtaken you except such as is common to man; but God is faithful, who will not allow you to be tempted beyond what you are able, but with the temptation will also make the way of escape, that you may be able to bear it" (1 Corinthians 10:13). "Wait on the LORD; be of good courage, and He shall strengthen your heart" (Psalm 27:14). Lord, enable my wife to endure temptation and receive the crown of life which You have promised to those who love You (James 1:12).

Give my wife patience while she is waiting for her prayers to be answered and for all things to be accomplished. Help her to wait upon You instead of waiting for things to change. Cause her to fear only You and to be content where she is this moment, knowing that You will not leave her there forever. Perfect her in Your "perfect love" that "casts out fear," so that fear has no room in her soul (1 John 4:18).

POWER TOOLS

GOD HAS NOT GIVEN US A SPIRIT OF FEAR, BUT OF POWER AND OF LOVE AND OF A SOUND MIND.

2 TIMOTHY 1:7

THERE IS NO FEAR IN LOVE; BUT PERFECT LOVE CASTS OUT FEAR, BECAUSE FEAR INVOLVES TORMENT. BUT HE WHO FEARS HAS NOT BEEN MADE PERFECT IN LOVE.

1 JOHN 4:18

THE FEAR OF MAN BRINGS A SNARE, BUT WHOEVER TRUSTS IN THE LORD SHALL BE SAFE.

PROVERBS 29:25

BLESSED IS THE MAN WHO ENDURES TEMPTATION; FOR WHEN HE HAS BEEN APPROVED, HE WILL RECEIVE THE CROWN OF LIFE WHICH THE LORD HAS PROMISED TO THOSE WHO LOVE HIM.

JAMES 1:12

I SOUGHT THE LORD, AND HE HEARD ME, AND DELIVERED ME FROM ALL MY FEARS.

PSALM 34:4

Chapter Thirteen

Her Purpose

Everyone has gifts and talents. Your wife needs to understand what hers are. That's because she will be truly fulfilled only when she is using the gifts God gave her, for the purpose for which God called her. If she doesn't understand what that purpose is, she will always have a certain amount of unrest and frustration. And that will affect your relationship in a subtle but important way.

Of course, a married woman's first call is to be a good wife to her husband. The Bible says that "an excellent wife is the crown of her husband" (Proverbs 12:4). We wives do want to be the crown that our husbands wear proudly. But too often the woman we are *called* to be and *want* to be—and know we *can* and *should* be—and the person we *are*, don't match up.

We try to be self-controlled, peaceful, serene, pleasant, strong, gracious, full of good humor, and attractive—all the things we know we have the potential to be and can clearly picture in our minds. But in weak moments—which happen with alarming regularity in a marriage relationship—our good intentions are overpowered by our flesh, and everything we have tried to build can be torn down by careless words and actions. We come face to face with the person we are at the moment, and we feel saddened and powerless to do anything about it.

Let's face it. None of us can be who we need to be without the power of God transforming us and enabling us to change. Marriage certainly won't transform any of us into a new person. However, wonderful changes *can* occur in us after we are married because now we are one with our mate and our prayers for one another have amazing new power. Miraculous things can happen. But often they don't because *we* try to make things happen in our mates instead of asking *God* to do it.

We can't force someone to be a certain way. That's why it's usually futile to demand that someone be different than he or she is. In fact, that kind of pressure can eventually ruin a relationship. But *praying* for your mate to become all she was created to be invites *God* to make changes that *last*. Putting the process of change entirely in the Lord's hands means you can trust that His timing and methods are perfect—and then you become free to enjoy the process.

Your wife *wants* to be the wife God created her to be and you need her to be. She wants to know how to best honor you and be a true helpmate. Pray for her to be able to do all that. And in the process, tell the Lord about any area of frustration you have. Be honest. Tell Him what you need more of (or less of) from your wife. If there's something you could change about her, what would it be? Tell God. Then ask Him to mold your requirements and her abilities into a mutually acceptable package.

No matter how good a wife she is, no matter how great a mother, no matter how perfectly she runs your home, your wife has other gifts and talents as well. These gifts are also part of who God made her to be. Whether she has used those gifts or not, they are there. Even if it has been years since she used them because she had to lay them aside to do other important things, they are still there. If you recognize her gifts, tell her what you see. What is obvious to you may not be obvious to her. She needs you to remind her that she was created for a high purpose. Don't let her deny who she is in order to try to become who she thinks you want. This will have serious consequences down the line. Pray that God will show her who He created her to be and enable her to become that.

Don't worry. This kind of praying will not threaten your marriage. Quite the contrary—it will enhance it. When you have a wife who is fulfilled because she is able to use her God-given gifts for His glory, it will be to your benefit. God will use her gifts in a way that is compatible with her being your wife and the mother of your children. God always makes our gifts fit into the life He has given us. Your wife's gifts will complement yours.

Another reason your wife needs to recognize her gifts and calling is so that she will not be seeking after something God is not calling her to be or do. That produces constant frustration and ultimate defeat. You would never take your favorite golf club and use it to drive nails into the deck of your home. That would be a grave misuse of the club because it would not be fulfilling the purpose for which the club was created. Your wife, too, can be hitting her head against a hard place if she doesn't discover the truth about who God made her to be. There will be a frustration in her that won't go away, and it may manifest itself as an unspoken resentment.

Women have a tendency to think that because they are mothers and have children at home, they have missed out on what God has called them to do. But this isn't true. It's in the doing of these immediate assignments God has given your wife that His ultimate purposes in her life will be realized. And there are ways for her to fulfill her calling even during the seasons of her life when not much time can be devoted to it. If your wife doesn't see how God's calling can ever be realized in the midst of her life as it now is, it's because she is trying to accomplish His purposes in her own strength. It must be *God* who does it all. Declaring her complete dependence on Him is the first step toward realizing His call on her life. Your prayers can help her to understand that.

In order to become all she was created to be, your wife needs love, support, and encouragement from you more than anyone else on earth. The richest, most famous, beautiful, successful, talented, acclaimed, and seemingly independent woman on earth still wants to know that her husband loves and values her. If she believes that he doesn't, she dies inside, no matter who else is singing her praises. Your prayers, as well as your words spoken to her, can help her to know how valuable she is to you. And when she knows that you love and appreciate her, it will give her life purpose like nothing else can.

SHE SAYS...

Please pray for your wife that:

1. She will understand God's purpose for her life.
2. She will recognize her gifts and talents.
3. She will be the wife God wants her to be.
4. She will be a wife deserving of honor and respect.
5. She will be the wife you need her to be.
6. She will use her gifts to help others.
7. She will fulfill God's call on her life.

HE SAYS...
BY MICHAEL HARRITON

Michael is a music composer. He and his wife, Terry, have been married for 23 years, and they have three grown children.

It's always tempting to eat from the tree of the knowledge of good and evil, the tree of judgment. We men feel so intelligent, so superior in our insight when with smug satisfaction we point out the flaws in our wives. But God has allowed us all to be flawed, and He uses our differences to complement one another. Instead of judging my wife for her emotionalism, for example, I try to remember that God has made my wife to be a *very sensitive barometer,* a very accurate gauge of what is really going on in my world. I wish I could say I heed her warnings all of the time. When I don't, I inevitably wish I had.

Just recently, my wife pointed out a situation in my business that she recognized was out of hand. She could see the dangers, but I couldn't see them at all. I thought she was flat-out wrong. In fact, I prayed for God to show my wife that she was in error. And as an afterthought, I prayed that if there was by any remote chance some deception or shortsightedness in me, God would remove it.

About two days later, the realization came flooding in on me that my wife was absolutely right and had been right all along. If I had not heeded her warning, the consequences could have been disastrous. These kinds of insights are unexpected fringe benefits of praying for our wives to be all God wants them to be. I pray for my wife to achieve 100 percent of her potential in Christ. (I also pray for myself that I would be healed of male pattern blindness.)

PRAYER POWER

Lord, I know that You have placed within (<u>wife's name</u>) special gifts and talents that are to be used for Your purpose and Your glory. Show her what they are, and show me too, Lord, that I may encourage her. Help her to know that You have something in particular for her to do and have given her a ministry that only she can fulfill. Give her a sense of Your call on her life, and open doors of opportunity for her to develop and use her gifts in that calling.

I pray that You would give my wife understanding that Your plan for her life has a specific and perfect timing. Even though she may not know the details of that plan, help her to rest in the confidence of knowing that You will bring it to pass as she seeks You in the details of her life.

Lord, I pray that (<u>wife's name</u>) will be the wife You have called her to be and the wife I need her to be. What I need most from my wife right now is (<u>name the need most pressing on your heart</u>). Show me what my wife needs from me. Help us to fulfill one another in these areas without requiring of each other more than we can be. Keep us from having unrealistic expectations of each other when our expectations should be in You. Help us to recognize the gifts You have placed in each of us and to encourage one another in their development and nurture.

Thank You, Lord, for the wife You have given me (Proverbs 19:14). Release her into Your perfect plan for her life so that she will fulfill the destiny You've given her. Use her gifts and talents to bless others.

Bring her into alignment with Your ultimate purpose for her life, and may she be fulfilled in it. I say to her, you are "like a fruitful vine in the very heart of your house" (Psalm 128:3). "Many daughters have done well, but you excel them all" (Proverbs 31:29). "Let your light so shine before men, that they may see your good works and glorify your Father in heaven" (Matthew 5:16). Lord, grant my wife according to her heart's desire, and fulfill all her purpose (Psalm 20:4).

POWER TOOLS

I...DO NOT CEASE TO GIVE THANKS FOR YOU, MAKING MEN-
TION OF YOU IN MY PRAYERS: THAT THE GOD OF OUR LORD
JESUS CHRIST, THE FATHER OF GLORY, MAY GIVE TO YOU
THE SPIRIT OF WISDOM AND REVELATION IN THE KNOWLEDGE
OF HIM, THE EYES OF YOUR UNDERSTANDING BEING
ENLIGHTENED; THAT YOU MAY KNOW WHAT IS THE HOPE OF
HIS CALLING, WHAT ARE THE RICHES OF THE GLORY OF HIS
INHERITANCE IN THE SAINTS, AND WHAT IS THE EXCEEDING
GREATNESS OF HIS POWER TOWARD US WHO BELIEVE,
ACCORDING TO THE WORKING OF HIS MIGHTY POWER.

EPHESIANS 1:15-19

THE GIFTS AND THE CALLING OF GOD ARE IRREVOCABLE.

ROMANS 11:29

...WHO HAS SAVED US AND CALLED US WITH A HOLY
CALLING, NOT ACCORDING TO OUR WORKS, BUT ACCORDING
TO HIS OWN PURPOSE AND GRACE WHICH WAS GIVEN TO US
IN CHRIST JESUS BEFORE TIME BEGAN.

2 TIMOTHY 1:9

IN HIM ALSO WE HAVE OBTAINED AN INHERITANCE, BEING
PREDESTINED ACCORDING TO THE PURPOSE OF HIM WHO
WORKS ALL THINGS ACCORDING TO THE COUNSEL OF HIS
WILL, THAT WE WHO FIRST TRUSTED IN CHRIST SHOULD BE
TO THE PRAISE OF HIS GLORY.

EPHESIANS 1:11,12

CHAPTER FOURTEEN

HER TRUST

Have you ever felt like your wife doesn't trust you? With finances? With taking care of your children? With that attractive woman at work? With important decisions? With your ability to hear from God?

If so, I'm sure it's not because she doesn't *want* to trust you. It's probably because her trust has been violated in the past. And not necessarily by you. Maybe her dad let her down. Or it could be that her first husband or boyfriend was untrustworthy. Or perhaps something you've done or *not* done, something you're not even aware of, has caused her to be hesitant to trust. Or maybe frightening things have happened to her because she trusted someone once. Or possibly her relationship with God is not as intimate as it could be, and she has not yet learned the safety of trusting *Him*. Whatever it is, ask the Lord to reveal it to both of you. You may discover something about yourselves that neither of you has ever realized. Something that could be healed through prayer.

Keep in mind that there are three extremely important areas in which a husband needs to be completely trustworthy. Failure in any one of these areas will cause his wife's trust to be weak in all the others.

1. *His absolute fidelity to his wife and his marriage.*

    There is nothing that violates trust like adultery. If a woman has been cheated on once, it changes her forever. She may forgive, but to forget, she would need a frontal lobotomy. Restoration takes a long time and requires a miraculous touch from God. Even if her husband has never actually done anything wrong, yet his actions around other women make her feel insecure about his ability to stay faithful to her in the future, then his wife cannot trust him.

2. *His responsibility to make a decent living and be wise with the family's finances.*

    No matter how much a man loves his wife and how well he treats her, if he is irresponsible with money, it undermines her faith in him. If, for example, he won't keep a steady job, so he is out of work most of the time while his family suffers. Or if his wife is the only one providing for the family, and this was not mutually agreed upon as their way of life. Or if he gambles away their money in any number of ways. In all such cases, his wife will feel that she cannot trust him.

3. *His consistent efforts to treat his wife and children with love and respect.*

    I know a number of women who can't trust their husbands to treat them and their children well. Although the husband is faithful and provides a good living, his wife never knows when he is going to explode in anger and be abusive over some insignificant thing. She simply can't trust him.

However, when a husband is consistently trustworthy in these three important areas, his wife finds it far easier to trust him in all the others. But trust must be *mutual* in a marriage. When one person can't or won't trust the other, neither of them can grow into all God has for them. That's why you also need to pray that *you* can trust your *wife*. "The heart of her husband safely trusts her; so he will have no lack of gain" (Proverbs 31:11). Much of the arguing and strife that goes on between marriage partners has to do with a lack of trust on the part of one or the other. The goal is to get to the point where both of you are so committed to the Lord that you can trust *Him* as He works in your mate.

Pray as well that God will give you the wisdom to lead your family and make right decisions. Often your wife's hesitancy about following you is not because she doesn't trust you, but rather because she trusts God more. She believes that only *He* knows certain things, and she wants to know that you have sought *Him* for wisdom and will make decisions based on *His* will. She needs to be certain that you have your future together as a family firmly in mind when you make all decisions. Pray that *your* trust in God will be so evident that *your wife* can in turn trust God to have her best interests at heart as He works through you.

Be patient in praying about this. Trust is broken quickly but takes time to restore. "Let us not grow weary while doing good, for in due season we shall reap if we do not lose heart" (Galatians 6:9). God *will* answer.

SHE SAYS...

Please pray for your wife that:

1. She will trust the Lord with her whole heart.
2. She will be able to completely trust you.
3. She will forgive anyone who has violated her trust.
4. You will be a trustworthy husband.
5. She will trust God working in you.
6. She will be a trustworthy wife.
7. She will be a woman of strong faith.

HE\SAYS...
BY RODNEY JOHNSON

Rodney is a real-estate agent. He and his wife, Valerie, have been married for 18 years, and they have three children.

Trust...how hard we strive for it and desire it in our relationships and how easily it is broken. As a real-estate agent in Los Angeles, I have experienced the extremes. One client so trusted me that he and his wife left me a $30,000 check made out to my company and gave me the power of attorney to buy them a particular million-dollar home if it became available while they went out of the country on a three-week vacation. On the other extreme, I had a client from outside the U.S. who was so suspicious of everything I did that ultimately she sabotaged the sale of one of the two homes she was trying to sell.

Guys, wouldn't you like your wife to be like the couple in my first example—willing to trust you to handle the finances, provide a home, and take her on her dream vacation without a care in the world? Sometimes, though, we all find ourselves thinking like the woman in my second example, who became suspicious of everyone and everything. If a woman is suspicious of a man, it is most likely because a male authority figure in her life has done something to break her trust. Now that I have been praying for my wife about this, our mutual trust has never been better.

Men, women need to know that they can trust us. The feminist movement notwithstanding, women want a man to lead, and they want to know that he can be trusted. Therefore, as you pray today for your wife's trust to grow, you must in turn pray to become more trustworthy yourself. If, for example, you have been doing things with the family finances secretively, without consulting your wife, this is a trust-buster. To win back her trust in this area, go to her with a repentant heart and a plan of action as to how you are going to change your untrustworthy behavior. Ultimately, you are a picture of our Father God to your wife and your children. If you can be trusted, it will be easier for your spouse and your kids to trust their heavenly Father.

PRAYER POWER

Lord, I pray that You would give (<u>wife's name</u>) the ability to trust me in all things. Most of all, I want her to trust Your Holy Spirit working in me and through me. Where I have not been worthy of that trust or have violated it, show me, and I will confess that before You as sin. Help me not to conduct myself that way anymore. Make me always be worthy of her trust. Show me how to convince her that I am in partnership with You and will do all I can to be trustworthy.

Where she has lost trust in me unjustly, I pray You would help her to see the truth. If she doesn't trust me because of something someone else has done to her, help her to forgive that person so she can be free. I pray that she will not project those failures onto me and expect that I will do the same thing. Specifically I pray about (<u>name any area where there is a lack of trust</u>).

In any place where we have broken trust with one another, help us to reestablish it as strong. May we both trust You, Lord, working in each of us. Break any unholy bonds or soul ties between me and any other woman in my past. Break any unholy bonds or soul ties between my wife and any other man in her past. Help us to fully repent of all relationships outside of our own that were not glorifying to You.

Lord, I pray that You would deepen my trust of my wife. Show me if there are places where I don't trust her judgment, her abilities, her loyalty, or her decisions. I pray that she will always be a trustworthy person and that I will be able to trust her completely.

Help me to be the kind of spiritual leader of our home and family that You want me to be. Increase our faith, for I know that You are a shield to those who put their trust in You (Proverbs 30:5). I say this day on behalf of my wife and me that You are our refuge and our fortress. You are our God, and in You will we trust (Psalm 91:2).

POWER TOOLS

AS FOR GOD, HIS WAY IS PERFECT; THE WORD OF THE LORD
IS PROVEN; HE IS A SHIELD TO ALL WHO TRUST IN HIM.

2 SAMUEL 22:31

TRUST IN THE LORD WITH ALL YOUR HEART, AND LEAN NOT
ON YOUR OWN UNDERSTANDING.

PROVERBS 3:5

LET ALL THOSE REJOICE WHO PUT THEIR TRUST IN YOU; LET
THEM EVER SHOUT FOR JOY, BECAUSE YOU DEFEND THEM;
LET THOSE ALSO WHO LOVE YOUR NAME BE JOYFUL IN YOU.
FOR YOU, O LORD, WILL BLESS THE RIGHTEOUS; WITH FAVOR
YOU WILL SURROUND HIM AS WITH A SHIELD.

PSALM 5:11,12

IT IS BETTER TO TRUST IN THE LORD THAN TO PUT CONFI-
DENCE IN MAN.

PSALM 118:8

LET HIM TRUST IN THE NAME OF THE LORD AND RELY UPON
HIS GOD.

ISAIAH 50:10

CHAPTER FIFTEEN

HER PROTECTION

In football, the perfect offense protects the quarterback from attack and frees him to do what he needs to do. He can either pass the ball to a receiver, hand off the ball to the running back, or run the ball to the goal line himself. This is exactly how your prayers of protection work for your wife. They create a strong wall around her so that no attack of the enemy can break through the lines to harm her. This allows her to do what she needs to do confidently and in safety. No matter what tricks the enemy has up his shoulder pads, they won't succeed.

So when your wife is out on the playing field of life facing a mean line of 350-pound demons, you as the captain can mobilize your team of angels through your prayers and see to it that she reaches the goal line without a scratch on her.

Now that our children are grown, I travel frequently on book tours and speaking engagements. But I wouldn't even consider leaving home without my husband praying over me for protection. In fact, I wouldn't be traveling at all if he weren't in agreement that I should be and then giving me his prayer support. And whenever *he* has to be out of town, he prays for my safety at home. (I do the same for him, but that's another book.)

There are few places completely safe anymore. Even in our own homes, evil and danger can intrude upon our lives with devastating swiftness. I knew a man who was killed in a car accident a few blocks from his home when he was coming back from the bank in the middle of the day. I knew a woman who was robbed and murdered when she pulled up in front of a neighbor's house to pick up her daughter from a Bible study. I know of a woman who was killed and whose car was then stolen, all in the parking lot of her local supermarket in the middle of the morning when she was getting groceries for her family. We can never take the safety of our loved ones for granted. Accidents happen suddenly and when we least expect them. It will give your wife the greatest comfort to know you are praying for her safety.

It's also important to pray for your wife to have good physical health. Taking care of her body is not easy for a woman. I don't know any woman who doesn't struggle with that in some way. And many women are almost blatantly negligent about it.

If someone were to present you with the car of your dreams, how would you take care of it? Would you neglect to have it serviced? Would you go out to the garage every day thinking, "What a waste of time to take care of this"? I know you wouldn't. Yet that's what your wife does to herself when she doesn't take care of her body. She may have many excuses, such as lack of time, lack of motivation, or lack of understanding about what to do, but your prayers can help her find the time, be motivated to do something, and gain the knowledge she needs.

Health decisions and body care can be complicated and confusing. There's an abundance of sometimes-conflicting information out there, and it makes us all want to go have a candy bar and forget the whole thing. But your prayers will have a positive effect on your wife's ability to hear God about what's right for her.

Permit me to again compare your wife to a car. (It's the only analogy that really speaks to my husband, so I've learned to communicate in these terms.) Your prayers will help your wife to value her chassis and keep it in good working order. They will enable her to exercise her engine enough to keep it in perfect running condition. They will help motivate her to keep up on the regular maintenance the owner's manual calls for, and not wait till she falls apart before she has a checkup. She won't think, "I'm just an old clunker, I'm not worth expensive repairs."

She needs your support in this area, but just talking to her about it won't work. You know how much good it does to go out and yell at your car when it needs to be serviced, and the same is true with your wife. If she is not taking care of herself properly, it's not because she doesn't want to. It's because she either doesn't know the correct things to do, doesn't realize the need for it, doesn't value herself enough, is too busy, or finds discipline in that area extremely difficult. She needs you to ask God to help her.

Tell her you are praying for her to have the strength, knowledge, wisdom, and motivation to take care of herself. And that you're doing it because she is the most valuable gift God has ever given you and you can't bear to see her sick. If she is a vintage model, all the more reason to pray that she will be completely restored.

If your wife is suffering from a specific health problem, ask God for healing. My husband has prayed for me for healing from so many different ailments over the past 30 years. But his finest hour of intercessory prayer came not long ago, when I felt something explode in my body and was doubled over in pain so excruciating that I knew I would die if a doctor didn't figure out the cause and do something about it quickly. It was three o'clock in the morning and Michael was the only one praying for me, except for me as I feebly groaned, "Help me, Jesus." I was completely dependent on my husband's prayers to move the hand of God and save my life. (He will tell you more about it at the end of this chapter.)

Our greatest efforts can't keep us well forever. Even on the best teams, the quarterback still gets sacked. God knew this, and that's why He sent Jesus as our Healer. So ask for healing on behalf of your wife. And don't stop praying until you see an answer. We can't afford to give up too soon when it comes to our health.

SHE SAYS...

Please pray for your wife that:

1. God will protect her body.
2. God will protect her mind and emotions.
3. She will have energy, strength, and endurance.
4. She will be motivated to take care of herself.
5. She will understand how to take care of her body.
6. She will be disciplined.
7. She will be protected wherever she goes.

HE SAYS...
BY MICHAEL OMARTIAN

My wife has the wonderful opportunity to travel and speak to women all over the country. I am painfully aware of the anxiety that creeps up on me at the thought of her getting on airplanes, going to strange towns and cities, staying in hotel rooms, dealing with bad food, being strained by many hours on her feet, and suffering normal anxiety over wanting to do well. There is no option for me but to pray over her before she goes and to continue to pray throughout the days that she is gone. But I have learned the importance of praying for her safety while she is home too.

At no time have my prayers ever been more urgent than when I was awakened at three o'clock one morning by the terrifying screams of my wife. She was doubled over in pain. She said she felt something had exploded within her. She's not one to complain, so I knew something was terribly wrong. The situation was so urgent, in fact, that we couldn't even take the time to wait for an ambulance. I was shaking as I managed to find her shoes and a warm coat to put over her pajamas. Our daughter Amanda and I helped a very doubled-over Stormie into our car, and I rushed down the freeway to the emergency hospital. I could do nothing to comfort her. She was in excruciating pain.

I knew enough to begin singing choruses of healing and praying fervently that she would be attended to immediately. When we arrived, I ran into the emergency admitting room, and thankfully a nurse was right there to rush to the car with a wheelchair. She sped Stormie into an examination room, and after a number of tests, a surgeon came and rushed her into surgery.

I prayed over her continuously, asking God to spare her life. I called others to pray, and they in turn called others as well. When the operation was completed and the surgeon came out to me, he said that her appendix had burst and she was dangerously close to death. He had been forced to take extreme measures to save her life, which meant the recovery would be long and difficult. It didn't matter. She was alive.

I have never experienced such fervency in praying as I learned that night. When we face a life-and-death issue it gives intercessory prayer new meaning. And I have never been so aware of the power and importance of my ongoing prayers for my wife's protection. All of those prayers for her safety over the years were answered. What if she had been out of town on a speaking engagement or on an airplane when that happened? It was God's grace and an answer to prayers for her protection that she wasn't.

PRAYER POWER

Lord, I pray that You would surround (<u>wife's name</u>) with Your hand of protection. Keep her safe from any accidents, diseases, or evil influences. Protect her in cars, planes, or wherever she is. Keep her out of harm's way.

Lord, You have said in Your Word that even though "the wicked watches the righteous, and seeks to slay him...[the] Lord will not leave him in his hand" (Psalm 37:32,33). Protect my wife from the plans of evil people. I pray that when she passes through deep waters, You will be with her, and when she passes through the rivers, they will not overflow her. When she walks through the fire, she shall not be burned nor shall the flame scorch her (Isaiah 43:2). I pray that (<u>wife's name</u>) will make her refuge "in the shadow of Your wings" until "these calamities have passed by" (Psalm 57:1).

Lord, I pray that You would help (<u>wife's name</u>) to truly see that her body is Your dwelling place. Enable her to be disciplined in the care of her body, and teach her to make right choices in what she eats. Give her the motivation to exercise regularly so that she has endurance. Help her to get plenty of rest so that she is completely rejuvenated when she awakens. May she acknowledge You in all her ways—including the care of her body—so that You can direct her paths.

Let no weapon formed against my wife be able to prosper (Isaiah 54:17). Keep her at all times under the umbrella of Your protection, and deliver her from the enemy's hand so no evil comes near her. Give Your angels charge over her to keep her in all her ways (Psalm 91:11). I say to my wife that God will "cover you with His feathers, and under His wings you shall take refuge; His truth shall be your shield and buckler. You shall not be afraid of the terror by night, nor of the arrow that flies by day, nor of the pestilence that walks in darkness, nor of the destruction that lays waste at noonday. A thousand may fall at your side, and ten thousand at your right hand; but it shall not come near you" (Psalm 91:4-7).

Thank You, Lord, that this day You will cover (<u>wife's name</u>) and help her to lie down in peace, and sleep; for You alone, O Lord, make her to dwell in safety (Psalm 4:8).

POWER TOOLS

THE LORD IS MY ROCK AND MY FORTRESS AND MY DELIV-
ERER; MY GOD, MY STRENGTH, IN WHOM I WILL TRUST; MY
SHIELD AND THE HORN OF MY SALVATION, MY STRONGHOLD.
I WILL CALL UPON THE LORD, WHO IS WORTHY TO BE
PRAISED; SO SHALL I BE SAVED FROM MY ENEMIES.

PSALM 18:2,3

BECAUSE YOU HAVE MADE THE LORD, WHO IS MY REFUGE,
EVEN THE MOST HIGH, YOUR DWELLING PLACE, NO EVIL
SHALL BEFALL YOU, NOR SHALL ANY PLAGUE COME NEAR
YOUR DWELLING; FOR HE SHALL GIVE HIS ANGELS CHARGE
OVER YOU, TO KEEP YOU IN ALL YOUR WAYS. IN THEIR
HANDS THEY SHALL BEAR YOU UP, LEST YOU DASH YOUR
FOOT AGAINST A STONE.

PSALM 91:9-12

I WILL RESTORE HEALTH TO YOU AND HEAL YOU OF YOUR
WOUNDS.

JEREMIAH 30:17

DO YOU NOT KNOW THAT YOUR BODY IS THE TEMPLE OF THE
HOLY SPIRIT WHO IS IN YOU, WHOM YOU HAVE FROM GOD,
AND YOU ARE NOT YOUR OWN? FOR YOU WERE BOUGHT AT A
PRICE; THEREFORE GLORIFY GOD IN YOUR BODY AND IN YOUR
SPIRIT, WHICH ARE GOD'S.

1 CORINTHIANS 6:19,20

THE PRAYER OF FAITH WILL SAVE THE SICK, AND THE LORD
WILL RAISE HIM UP.

JAMES 5:15

CHAPTER SIXTEEN

HER DESIRES

The last person I ever desired to marry was a man addicted to football, who had to spend his evenings and weekends on the couch listening to every sports channel. That's why one of the things that I found most attractive about Michael when we were dating was that he claimed to have no interest whatsoever in televised sports. So it was quite shocking to me when, a few years into our marriage, Michael not only became interested in sports, he became obsessed. He dressed in Bears T-shirts and Cubs hats. He screamed in front of the TV until everyone around him was deaf. He took me to a few games, but I thought it was ridiculous to see a bunch of grown men falling all over each other, fighting over a ball that wasn't even round. The hot dogs held more interest for me. I was upset that I had been deceived before the wedding.

Once I learned to pray for my husband the way God wanted me to (as I shared in *The Power of a Praying Wife*), God gave me a new perspective on this situation. But for some unfathomable reason, He did not take away my husband's obsession for sports like I had prayed. Instead Michael and I came to an agreement that I would not look upon his avid interest in football with disdain and disrespect if he would not pressure me to feign interest in it.

This truce was tolerable, and the practicality of it was livable for quite some time. But Michael wasn't content with that, and so he started praying for me behind my back. He prayed that I would go to football games with him once in a while and actually enjoy it. He knew this was a lot to ask of God, but He *had* parted the Red Sea and all.

For some amazing reason, one day my eyes were suddenly opened and I got a picture of what the game was about and how fascinating it was. The thrill of a completed pass. The utter disappointment when the quarterback is sacked. The art form of precision teamwork. The joy of an unexpected play that the other team isn't prepared to stop. Now I never miss a game, and I don't even care about the hot dogs.

Is there an interest you wish your wife would share with you? Pray for her to develop that interest. Obviously, nothing is impossible with God. He can even open your wife's eyes to the thrills and wonders of your favorite pastime. All she needs is a little prayer. But there is more to pray about than just interests and activities. There are dreams and desires that should be prayed about too.

Everyone has dreams. Some of them come from our flesh, but many are put in our hearts by God. It's vitally important to know which is which, because it is miserable when we mistake our own dreams for *His*. When we pursue our own dreams and make idols out of them, we become unfulfilled. When we *don't* pursue the ones *He* gives us, we become bitter.

It's not that God doesn't want us to dream. He does. God says we can't live without a dream or vision. But He doesn't want us to leave *Him* out of it. And if the dream we are dreaming is not from the Lord, we will be forever frustrated by the fact that it is never realized. He wants us to surrender our dreams to Him. When we do that, it will seem as if they are completely dead. But God will resurrect the ones that are from Him and release us from the ones that are not.

It's amazing how we can live in the same house with a person for years and never know the deepest desire of his or her heart. And all because we don't ask. Often our dreams and desires are so deep that we don't even verbalize them. Or we believe that the possibility of them ever happening is so remote that we lose hope.

I know a woman who had the deepest desire to travel and see other interesting places. She was married to a husband with a very strong and controlling personality. He was the CEO of his company, and business was his life. He devoted himself to it without a moment's thought about what her dream or desire was. He wasn't a bad man. He was actually a good man who had never inquired about his wife's dream. He only thought about *his,* and he was living it.

His wife was lonely and unfulfilled, and her children were grown-up and didn't need her much anymore. So she often sat alone with travel magazines and books and soap operas, and dreamed of another life. One day, another married man looked into her eyes and saw *her.* He wanted to know what she thought and what her dreams were. It turned into an affair that nearly destroyed both marriages. When it all came to light, it was a major wake-up call for her husband. Determined to save the marriage, they both went to Christian marriage counseling. To the husband's credit, he confessed that he had been neglectful of his wife, and he started to really listen to the cries of her heart. They began to travel together to wonderful places, fulfilling her lifelong dream. Their marriage was eventually healed, but it took years of gut-wrenching struggle to repair it.

I know another woman who has artistic talent, and had a dream of painting pictures that were worthy of the finest walls. She was sinking daily from the frustration of unfulfillment of it. When her wise husband asked her about the dream or desire of her heart, she shared all that with him. He prayed with her about it, and she released her desire to the Lord. Soon after that, he suggested that she take an art class while he watched their two small children. It changed her life. She bought art supplies for herself and her children, and the three of them painted together every day. To be able to express the gift within her and fulfill a desire she'd had released her so much that it gave new purpose and energy to her personality.

Sometimes the answers to life's frustrations are so simple. As simple as asking a loved one about her dream and then praying it into existence or completely out of her life. Husbands, if you want a happy and fulfilled wife who is a joy to be around, ask her if there is a dream deep within her heart that she longs to see fulfilled. Listen openly as she describes it, with no judgment, no condemnation, and no lecture on why it's not possible. Then pray for her to be able to surrender it to the Lord. When she is able to surrender her dream to God, He will either take the desire for it away or else bring it to full fruition in His way and in His time. Either way, she will find peace.

If the dream your wife shares with you is of the Lord and He opens a door, encourage her to walk through it. If her dream is not of God, He will use your prayers to release her into something far better and more rewarding. And the rewards of a released wife are ones you will thank me for later on.

SHE SAYS...

Please pray for your wife that:

1. She will know if the dreams in her heart are from God.
2. She will be able to share her dreams with you.
3. Her dreams will be compatible with yours.
4. She will take an interest in what interests you.
5. The two of you will have interests you share together.
6. She will be able to surrender her dreams to the Lord.
7. She will have the desires of her heart.

HE SAYS...
BY MICHAEL OMARTIAN

Oh no, she's going to give me that look again, I thought. *That look that says, "Do you ever get enough of sitting in front of that stupid TV watching football?"* Of course my answer was, "Why no, dear, you know I'm just a Neanderthal kind of guy whose interests never drift beyond caveman pursuits." I would endure the look, feeling that the possibility of her ever approving of this "waste of time," let alone sharing it, was beyond the scope of possibility. I now know better!

A simple prayer—and I mean *simple*—was all that it took, and 27 years of football disapproval was replaced by an enthusiasm I never thought possible and I'm not sure I want at this point! Stormie is now a Tennessee Titan fan to the max. She has the sweatshirts, the T-shirts, the hats, and she screams when the action gets close. She even raves about her favorite players on the team. There might have been a time when I would have felt threatened by such declarations, but now I'm just too tired to put up a fight. And besides, it's fun to go to games with my enthusiastic wife. Another amazing answer to prayer. Who would have thought it possible?

I have also prayed for her about her dream of seeing the books she has written go all over the world. They have now been translated into 11 languages. As she says, this has gone beyond her wildest dreams. Only God can do that. And I know I had a part in it because I prayed.

Prayer Power

Lord, I pray that You would touch (<u>wife's name</u>) this day and fulfill her deepest desires. Help her to surrender her dreams to You so that You can bring to life the ones You have placed in her heart. I pray that she will never try to follow a dream of her own making, one that You will not bless. Help her to surrender *her* plans so that You can reveal *Your* plan. I know that in Your plan, timing is everything. May she reach for her highest dreams in Your perfect timing.

Lord, I pray that in the midst of all my wife has to do, there would be time for what she enjoys most. Help me understand the things that interest her. I also pray that You would make a way for us to share (<u>name a specific activity or interest you would like to do together</u>). Help her to understand my enjoyment of it, and may she develop an appreciation for it too. Show me how to encourage her in this area. Give me words without any negative undertones that will inspire her. If this is not an appropriate activity for us, show us one that would be. I pray we will have common interests we can enjoy together.

Lord, I know that You would not give us dreams that aren't compatible. I pray that the desires of our hearts will be perfectly knitted together. May we not only be caught up in our own dreams but in each other's as well. Help us to always share with one another the deepest desires of our hearts.

POWER TOOLS

DELIGHT YOURSELF ALSO IN THE LORD, AND HE SHALL GIVE YOU THE DESIRES OF YOUR HEART.

PSALM 37:4

HE WILL FULFILL THE DESIRE OF THOSE WHO FEAR HIM; HE ALSO WILL HEAR THEIR CRY AND SAVE THEM.

PSALM 145:19

WHERE THERE IS NO VISION, THE PEOPLE PERISH.

PROVERBS 29:18 KJV

YOU OPEN YOUR HAND AND SATISFY THE DESIRE OF EVERY LIVING THING.

PSALM 145:16

THEY CRY OUT TO THE LORD IN THEIR TROUBLE, AND HE BRINGS THEM OUT OF THEIR DISTRESSES. HE CALMS THE STORM, SO THAT ITS WAVES ARE STILL. THEN THEY ARE GLAD BECAUSE THEY ARE QUIET; SO HE GUIDES THEM TO THEIR DESIRED HAVEN.

PSALM 107:28-30

CHAPTER SEVENTEEN

HER WORK

The perfect woman, according to the Bible, is a hard worker. This woman creates, manages, and provides. She buys and sells property (a real-estate agent?). She plants a vineyard (a gardener?). She makes clothing (a seamstress?). And she sells it (a retailer?). She is a woman of strength, energy, and vision, who works into the night and knows that what she has to offer is good. In the midst of it all, she takes care of her family, gives to the poor, and makes her husband proud. He is blessed by the excellence of all she does (Proverbs 31). If this is what your wife aspires to, she needs your help. Frankly, I'm exhausted just reading about it.

Every woman works. But some are more appreciated for what they do than others. Many wives work because they want to contribute financially to the family. Many work simply because they enjoy what they do. Others have abilities that are valuable to people who are willing to pay for them. For many women, maintaining a home and raising children *is* their work. And they take it seriously and want to do it well. For other women, ministry opportunities or volunteer activities are their work. No matter what the particulars of your wife's work, it gives her fulfillment and the satisfaction of accomplishment if it makes life better for her, her family, or someone else. But she needs your prayers and support.

Don't be hesitant to encourage your wife to be all she can be in her work. It won't mean that she will no longer need you when she is successful. In fact, quite the opposite. It will cause her to need you even more. If you support your woman in prayer, she will not get arrogant and cocky when the blessings roll in. She will not think, "Look how great I am. I don't need him. Why, I can do better without him." That's what women think who are married to men who *don't* encourage and support them in prayer. Your wife will never become so complete that she doesn't need you. Her success will never undermine your position in her life. It will elevate it. Your prayers will mean so much to her that she will become "addicted" to them. Remember, the two of you are one and what happens to her happens to you. You need never feel intimidated by her success.

Because my husband is a producer in the music business, we have come to know many women who have had phenomenal success. The couples who have been able to see this success as a blessing from God for them both have dealt with it the best. The husbands who have resented their wife's success have destroyed the marriage. Limiting a woman's potential will destroy her. That's why her achievements must be covered in prayer.

A woman needs to have a sense of accomplishment, just like a man does. However, if a man doesn't have it, he feels like a failure. If a woman doesn't have it, she experiences frustration and unfulfillment. This will in turn affect all the other areas of her life—especially her relationship with her husband. A woman whose work is raising children and running a successful home still needs that sense of accomplishment and the recognition for a job well done. Unlike her sisters in the workplace, the only one she can really hear that affirmation from is her husband. That's why his prayers for her are so important. They breed affirmation.

No matter what kind of work your wife does, she needs your prayers and encouragement, and God's guidance and blessings. Pray for her to find that perfect balance of confidence in her abilities but total reliance upon the Lord to enable her to do what she needs to do.

SHE SAYS...

Please pray for your wife that:

1. She will glorify the Lord in her work.
2. She will do her work well.
3. She will be respected for the work she does.
4. She will be compensated well for her work.
5. She will have strength to get her work done.
6. You will approve of her work.
7. Her work will bring fulfillment to her.

HE SAYS...
BY MICHAEL OMARTIAN

I remember that early in our marriage, during our child-raising years, Stormie expressed the desire to write books. She had written the lyrics to many songs, and we collaborated frequently. She was comfortable with writing songs since it required only a relatively small time commitment, but she felt strongly that to sacrifice time to write a book, time that would be spent away from raising the children, was out of the question. That impressed me to no end. I began praying that God would bless her more than she could imagine for her faithfulness to our children in their early years.

Psalm 37:4 says, "Delight yourself also in the LORD, and He shall give you the desires of your heart." My wife delighted herself in the fulfilling of the responsibilities God had given to her. My prayer was for her to have strength and patience. When the children were older and she had more time available, God gave her the desire of her heart to write books. Of course, I prayed her through each one. Now she is the author of many successful books, and God has blessed her work because she relied on Him every step of the way.

PRAYER POWER

Lord, I pray that You would help (<u>wife's name</u>) to be successful in her work. No matter what her work is at any given time, establish it, and help her to find favor. Thank You for the abilities, gifts, and creativity You have placed in her. Continue to reveal, develop, and refine those gifts and talents, and use them for Your purposes. May her skills increase in value, and may she excel in each of them. Open doors for her that no man can shut, and bless her with success.

Keep us from ever being in competition with one another, and help us to always rejoice in each other's accomplishments. Help us to build one another up and not forget that we are on the same team. If what she is doing is not in Your perfect will, show her what Your will is. Keep pride far from her so that the enemy will never be able to make her fall. Show me how I can encourage her.

Lord, Your Word says when we commit our work to You, the financial blessing we receive will not bring misery along with it (Proverbs 10:22). You have also said "the laborer is worthy of his wages" (1 Timothy 5:18). I pray that (<u>wife's name</u>) will be rewarded well for her labor and that it will bless us, our family, and others. Give her the gift of work that she loves and establish the work of her hands (Psalm 90:17). Enable her to accomplish great things so that You are glorified.

POWER TOOLS

LET THE BEAUTY OF THE LORD OUR GOD BE UPON US, AND ESTABLISH THE WORK OF OUR HANDS FOR US; YES, ESTABLISH THE WORK OF OUR HANDS.

PSALM 90:17

THE LABOR OF THE RIGHTEOUS LEADS TO LIFE.

PROVERBS 10:16

THIS BOOK OF THE LAW SHALL NOT DEPART FROM YOUR MOUTH, BUT YOU SHALL MEDITATE IN IT DAY AND NIGHT, THAT YOU MAY OBSERVE TO DO ACCORDING TO ALL THAT IS WRITTEN IN IT. FOR THEN YOU WILL MAKE YOUR WAY PROSPEROUS, AND THEN YOU WILL HAVE GOOD SUCCESS.

JOSHUA 1:8

HE WHO HAS A SLACK HAND BECOMES POOR, BUT THE HAND OF THE DILIGENT MAKES RICH.

PROVERBS 10:4

IN ALL LABOR THERE IS PROFIT, BUT IDLE CHATTER LEADS ONLY TO POVERTY.

PROVERBS 14:23

CHAPTER EIGHTEEN

HER DELIVERANCE

Picture yourself out sailing on a beautiful, clear, sunny day. A gentle wind is blowing in your face and rustling the sails. The water is calm as you glide along peacefully. You sense the open sea giving you life. You can feel it seeping through your pores and into your innermost being. You have a renewed sense that life is good. You can relax and enjoy the moment as you sail to your destination.

Carefree sailing like that only happens when it's done right. The sails have to be positioned perfectly to catch the wind so the boat can move forward. If they don't catch the wind properly, the boat can be tossed unpredictably. You can end up going around in circles revisiting the same old territory, and never actually getting anywhere. Or worse yet, you can lose control and capsize.

The same is true for us. If we are not positioned right in our relationship to the Lord, we never catch that wind of His Spirit that enables us to sail against the tide of our limitations and circumstances and arrive at our destination. We keep coming back to the same old places, and we never get free. And the ride can get rough and unpleasant. We sometimes lose control and get the feeling that we're sinking. But when we move with the Spirit of God, He never leaves us to wander around where we are. He moves us on to where we are supposed to be.

The problem is, we can't move on to where we are supposed to be if we have dropped anchor in the past. Whether it's something that happened 30 years ago or only as recently as yesterday, the past can keep us where we are if we don't pull in our anchor. God wants us to sail freely. He wants us to leave those old broken places behind so we can become whole people. This is especially important in a marriage, because that's where the mirror of our lives is held up to us daily. We see what we're made of, good or bad, moment by moment. The more whole we are individually, the better our marriages will be. But if we don't seek that fresh wind of God's Spirit to carry us, we never arrive at that place of wholeness and peace.

MOVING AWAY FROM HURTS
OF THE PAST

No matter what your wife's past is, unless she has been able to step out of it, she won't be able to live successfully in the present or move into the future God has for her. Whatever hurt from the past that your wife has brought into your marriage will affect the present and the future of your life together. It could be something that someone said or did to her, or the trauma of things that happened to her, or something she did herself. Whatever it is, if it keeps her from having peace about the past, present, or future of her life, then she needs to get free of it. And she needs your prayers to help her do that.

After I wrote the book *Stormie* about my life of devastation and the road I took to find total restoration in the Lord, I received countless letters from men married to women who had come from abusive or emotionally damaging childhoods. In each case, the woman seemed fine when the man married her, but after they were married she fell apart. The husband felt helpless in the face of the depression and turmoil his wife was going through and was at a loss as to how to help her. Her emotional swings were too confusing for him. He didn't feel up to the task at hand, even if he could figure out what it was. He found it impossible to relate to what his wife was experiencing. This is what I advised each one of those men:

"Because of the love you have for your wife, and the fact that you have committed yourself to her in marriage, you have provided a safe haven for her," I wrote. "Your love tangibly represents God's love. She now feels loved enough and safe enough to face the frightening issues of the past and let them be exposed to the healing light of God's presence and power so she can be released from them. She feels secure enough to fall apart so that the Lord can put her back together again. What she wants from you is to know you will continue to stand by her with love and support—even if you don't fully understand what she's feeling or going through. She needs your prayer covering because it will 'break the back' of the enemy and provide a place of protection while she heals."

THE NEED FOR FORGIVENESS

We can never sail smoothly out of our past and into the future God has for us without forgiveness. That's because our greatest hurts usually come from people. If there are negative relationships in your wife's past (especially old boyfriends, or an ex-husband), pray for her to be delivered from the effects of them so she won't bring ghosts from the past into your life together now. Those ghosts can appear at your most intimate times together without your even knowing what's happening. You don't want to be constantly trying to prove that you are not like the person with whom she had a bad experience before she knew you.

Another important area of healing to pray about is your wife's relationship to her earthly father. The way he treated her will affect how she relates both to God and to you. Was he strong and there for her? Did he abandon or abuse her? If she had a father who molested or mistreated her, or who made her feel bad about herself in some way, she may have a hard time trusting you. It's not that she doesn't want to, it's just that the man who was *supposed* to protect and love her didn't. If she doubted her earthly father's love, she may doubt her heavenly Father's love, which may cause her to doubt your love as well. This is where your prayers can make a major difference.

There are also traumatic events that can affect a woman so profoundly that she needs prayer to get free from the memory of them. For example, I once witnessed a man bleed to death after a terrible car accident. I didn't see the accident happen, but I drove by immediately afterward and stopped to help and report it on my cell phone. The man was alone and trapped in his car, and as I prayed I saw the life drain out of him before the ambulance even arrived. It was so traumatic for me that I had nightmares for days afterward. My husband finally had to pray for me to be delivered from the grip of that memory, and then the nightmares stopped.

FINDING FREEDOM

We all need to get free of anything that binds us. It could be anger, resentment, bitterness, or depression. The number of women who struggle with depression is staggering. But God doesn't want women struggling with any of these things. He wants them to be set free. If your wife is tormented by depression, for example, she needs you to stand with her in prayer until she receives freedom from it, no matter how long it takes.

The struggle many women have with food is a deep and troubling problem for them, one that requires deliverance. They desperately need their husbands to pray for them until they find victory in this tormenting issue.

The great thing about praying for your wife to get free is that *you* don't have to have all the answers. She's not expecting that anyway. And you don't have to understand everything. She may not even understand it herself. But God understands everything and has all the answers, so put *Him* in charge. Your wife just wants to know that you will continue to love and support her when you see what she's been holding inside.

If you have a wife who needs a lot of freedom and healing, you may be thinking, "I don't have it in me to deal with all of my wife's problems. I just want to sail along peacefully, and she's stirring up the waters." But that's why opposites attract—so they can complete each other. Do you have any idea how boring it would be to live with someone who was exactly like you? Where would the spark be? The challenge? You would be able to predict your wife's every word, her every move, because it would be the same as what *you* would say or do.

I'll never forget the time I was involved in a seminar where the host and hostess divided us into personality groups. The outgoing people who needed to be the center of attention were all together. The sensitive, deeply thoughtful people were all put together, and so on. It was completely miserable. The outgoing people were constantly

trying to outdo one another. The sensitive, deeply thoughtful people were depressing each other. I couldn't wait to get
back into a mixed group. Being exactly alike is boring.

You may be thinking that you would gladly trade all the
excitement you've been having for a little more boredom.
And I understand that. But when we are challenged by our
mate's problems, it makes us stretch. So even though your
wife may be going through a difficult time that seems like
more than you have the patience to bear, just remember
how privileged you are to be an instrument of God's healing,
and thank Him for allowing you to grow along with her.

THE DELIVERANCE PROCESS

The most startling thing I discovered about being preg-
nant was that from the moment I conceived, a process was
set in motion. And there was no way I could stop it, outside of doing something that would terminate it. It was
entirely out of my control. The process was going to go on,
with or without my cooperation. That sense of being completely out of control of your body is a strange feeling.
Sometimes that's exactly the way the deliverance process
feels. It's going on whether you want it to or not. But that's
because you have submitted your life to the Lord, and He
wants you to be free. When God decides you are ready to
go through it, He plants the seed, and it becomes a force
that grows until you give birth to freedom. And just as with
delivering a baby, there's a certain amount of pain that is a
part of the deliverance process. But when it's over, you're
glad you went through it.

Emotional hurts and bondage usually come off in layers,
just the way they got there in the first place. That's why,
even though your wife may have achieved a breakthrough

in a certain area, the whole thing may come back with even greater force. It will appear to be the same old thing all over again, only worse this time. If that happens, don't be intimidated or disappointed by it. Don't think that things are getting worse instead of better. It just means that there are new layers of hurt or bondage that are coming to the surface for healing, and that God is leading your wife into a deeper level of deliverance. Often the deepest layers are the most painful. Just cling to God in the midst of the storm, and He will bring you through it safely.

Just as with giving birth to a baby, the worst pain comes right before the greatest deliverance of our lives. Things are the most difficult right before the biggest blessing is about to come forth. But God's timing is perfect. If women were able to deliver babies whenever *we* wanted to, we would deliver them sometime in the second month when the morning sickness kicked in. But the baby would not survive because it would be premature. The same is true with deliverance. We have to provide the best conditions we can, give it time, and try not to do anything to terminate it once the process has been set in motion.

Only God has the kind of love that can calm the storms of our lives. Only He can set our sails and move us in the right direction. Pray that your wife can pull up the anchor from her past and allow the fresh, calm wind of the Holy Spirit to get her sailing smoothly where she needs to go.

SHE SAYS...

Please pray for your wife that:

1. She will find deliverance and freedom in the Lord.
2. Nothing will separate her from all God has for her.
3. She will have emotional and mental wholeness.
4. She will be able to release the past completely.
5. She will forgive anyone she needs to forgive.
6. You will always love and support her in prayer.
7. Her life will become a testimony of God's healing power.

HE SAYS...
BY NEIL T. ANDERSON

Neil is the president of Freedom in Christ Ministries and author of Victory Over the Darkness *and* The Bondage Breaker. *He and his wife, Joanne, have been married for 33 years, and they have two children and two grandchildren.*

In the spring of 1986 my wife had eye surgery to replace a defective lens. It should have been a fairly routine surgery, but Joanne did not respond well to the anesthetic. She suffered a phobic condition, which led to a major depression lasting 15 months. Nothing her doctors did reduced her symptoms. In the midst of it, I got caught in a major role conflict. Was I her pastor, discipler, or counselor (which I had been for many people)? Or was I her husband? I realized I could only be the latter. I was in a situation I could not fix or control.

During this trial we lost everything we had. We were stripped down to nothing, and I realized for the first time that if God is all I have, then God is all I need. My ministry was to hold onto Joanne every day and say, "This too will pass." And it did pass, through prayer and humble dependence on God. The Lord brought me to the end of *my* resources so I could discover *His*. It's only God who can bind up the brokenhearted and set the captive free. Out of this period of brokenness, Freedom in Christ Ministries was born. And our marriage has been greatly strengthened.

PRAYER POWER

Lord, I pray that You would set (<u>wife's name</u>) free from anything that holds her other than You. Deliver her from any memory of the past that has the power to control her or keep her trapped in its grip. Help her to forgive any person who has hurt her so that unforgiveness will not be able to hold her captive.

Set (<u>wife's name</u>) free from everything that keeps her from being all You created her to be. Keep her protected from the plans of the enemy so that he cannot thwart the deliverance and healing You want to bring about in her life. Restore all that has been stolen from her until she is lacking no good thing. I know that in Your presence is healing and wholeness. Help her to live in Your presence so that she can be made totally whole.

Lord, I know that "though we walk in the flesh, we do not war according to the flesh. For the weapons of our warfare are not carnal but mighty in God for pulling down strongholds" (2 Corinthians 10:3,4). In the name of Jesus I pull down any strongholds the enemy has erected around (<u>wife's name</u>). Specifically I pray that my wife will be set free from (<u>name a specific area of struggle from which your wife needs to find freedom</u>). Set her free from this in the name of Jesus. I pray that for her sake You "will not rest, until her righteousness goes forth as brightness, and her salvation as a lamp that burns" (Isaiah 62:1). Make darkness light before her "and crooked places straight" (Isaiah 42:16). You have said in Your Word that "whoever walks wisely will be delivered" (Proverbs 28:26). I pray she will walk with wisdom and find full deliverance. Show me how to love and support her well in the process.

POWER TOOLS

DO NOT REMEMBER THE FORMER THINGS, NOR CONSIDER THE THINGS OF OLD. BEHOLD, I WILL DO A NEW THING, NOW IT SHALL SPRING FORTH; SHALL YOU NOT KNOW IT? I WILL EVEN MAKE A ROAD IN THE WILDERNESS AND RIVERS IN THE DESERT.

ISAIAH 43:18,19

THE LORD WILL DELIVER ME FROM EVERY EVIL WORK AND PRESERVE ME FOR HIS HEAVENLY KINGDOM. TO HIM BE GLORY FOREVER AND EVER.

2 TIMOTHY 4:18

...YOU HAVE HEARD HIM AND HAVE BEEN TAUGHT BY HIM, AS THE TRUTH IS IN JESUS: THAT YOU PUT OFF, CONCERNING YOUR FORMER CONDUCT, THE OLD MAN WHICH GROWS COR-RUPT ACCORDING TO THE DECEITFUL LUSTS, AND BE RENEWED IN THE SPIRIT OF YOUR MIND, AND THAT YOU PUT ON THE NEW MAN WHICH WAS CREATED ACCORDING TO GOD, IN TRUE RIGHTEOUSNESS AND HOLINESS.

EPHESIANS 4:21-24

IF ANYONE IS IN CHRIST, HE IS A NEW CREATION; OLD THINGS HAVE PASSED AWAY; BEHOLD, ALL THINGS HAVE BECOME NEW.

2 CORINTHIANS 5:17

FORGETTING THOSE THINGS WHICH ARE BEHIND AND REACHING FORWARD TO THOSE THINGS WHICH ARE AHEAD, I PRESS TOWARD THE GOAL FOR THE PRIZE OF THE UPWARD CALL OF GOD IN CHRIST JESUS.

PHILIPPIANS 3:13,14

CHAPTER NINETEEN

HER OBEDIENCE

One year my husband bought me a set of golf clubs and a series of golf lessons as a Christmas gift. I took the lessons and learned how frustrating it was to try to hit a ball that was so small it was impossible to even find it in a patch of weeds. And I wondered why on earth grown men would spend hours doing this every week. That is, until one day I went out to the golf course, placed my ball on the tee at the first hole, gripped my driver, eyed the fairway, looked down at that tiny ball, and did everything in my swing that I had learned how to do. When the head of my club connected squarely with the ball, there was the most glorious sound. It was like nothing else I'd ever heard, except for maybe the sound of Sammy Sosa's bat hitting a home run at Wrigley Field. My swing was completely right, and the ball sailed straight down the fairway for 170 yards. In that instant I understood why men spend so much time on the golf course. They want to hear that sound. They want to experience how it feels to do it right.

That's the same way it is with obedience. You get the most wonderful feeling when you know that you have just obeyed God and it pleases Him. It's seeing that, when you do things God's way, the right way, life works. That feeling keeps you coming back and trying harder, because you want to do whatever it takes to experience it.

The greatest thing we feel when we obey God is a deeper sense of His presence. That's because there is a link between obedience and our experience of the presence of God. Jesus said, "If anyone loves me, he will keep my word; and my Father will love him, and we will come to him and make our home with him" (John 14:23). He manifests Himself to those who love and obey Him. So often we sacrifice the *fullness* of His presence operating in our lives because of disobedience. Your wife longs to feel that fullness of God's presence on a regular basis. She wants to experience the thrilling sense of God's pleasure when she has obeyed Him. She needs you to pray that she will consistently be able to live God's way.

No matter what game you are playing, there are consequences and penalties for not playing by the rules. One of the consequences for disobedience is not getting our prayers answered (Proverbs 28:9, Psalm 66:18). You don't want your wife to neglect some of the rules and not get her prayers answered. Pray for the eyes of her understanding to be enlightened so that she is clear about the rules of the game.

One of the most common ways women can be disobedient is with our speech. The Bible is very clear on this subject.

- *We are not to be too quick to speak.* "Do you see a man hasty in his words? There is more hope for a fool than for him" (Proverbs 29:20).
- *We are not to say everything we feel, when we feel like it.* "A fool vents all his feelings, but a wise man holds them back" (Proverbs 29:11).

- *Our words can destroy people.* "Death and life are in the power of the tongue, and those who love it will eat its fruit" (Proverbs 18:21).
- *Timing is everything.* "The heart of the righteous studies how to answer, but the mouth of the wicked pours forth evil" (Proverbs 15:28).

Most women love to talk. That's because nearly any woman is overflowing with thoughts, feelings, emotions, revelations, insights, hurts, and joys, and it feels as if she will burst if she does not share them with someone. Out of the overflow of her heart her mouth speaks, and some women overflow more than others.

Communication is a woman's greatest joy. It also can be one of her greatest assets. By her speech alliances are formed, emotions are healed, knowledge is imparted, relationships are restored, mysteries are unraveled, and world problems are solved. She loves to talk things out. Show me a woman who will not talk, and I'll show you a woman who has had people in her life who never listened to what she had to say.

Every woman is well aware of the power of her words and what a long-lasting effect they can have (after all, a wife remembers things her husband said years ago, which he forgot 30 seconds afterward). She agonizes over words she has spoken if she thinks they may have hurt someone. If she says something that is interpreted differently than what she intended, or if she speaks too harshly to her children or to a friend, she has deep regrets. That's why women have specifically asked to be prayed for in this area. Your wife needs your prayers that God will create in her a clean heart and give her words that edify and bring life. She needs discernment from God about what to say and when to say it. And she needs to recognize when it is time to keep silent.

No woman wants to be a complainer, but in her attempt to make life good for her husband, her children, herself, and others, she often sees things that are wrong and tries to change them with her words. If you ever find your wife saying the same thing over and over to you out of the frustration of her heart, pray with her about it. It will give her peace to know that you understand her concern well enough to put it in a prayer. And she'll feel relieved knowing that you have committed it to God. She may even stop talking about it.

Speaking words that bring life is only one of *many* areas of obedience. Your wife wants you to pray that she will be able to do well in *all* of them. She wants to get to the point in her walk with God that she can hit those perfect long drives down the fairway of her life without a slice or a hook. She may not always hit a hole in one, but at least she won't end up in any of those embarrassing sand traps either. Pray for her to hear that wonderful sound of God's voice saying, "Well done, good and faithful servant."

SHE SAYS...

Please pray for your wife that:

1. She will have a heart to obey God.
2. She will understand what God requires of her.
3. She will choose to live God's way.
4. The Holy Spirit will control her actions.
5. Her words will always edify and bring life.
6. God will help her to obey Him.
7. She will please God by her obedience.

HE SAYS...
BY MICHAEL OMARTIAN

My wife has a heart to obey God. But it's not always easy. Sometimes there are choices to be made and it's not clear what God wants her to do. She asks me to pray that she will hear God's voice and have His leading about which way to walk. I also pray for her to have the strength to stand strong and not slack off in her obedience to the things she already knows to do. I pray that the Holy Spirit will lead her in all things so that obedience comes naturally.

One time in particular I felt that God was leading us to move to a different state. My wife did not feel that leading and said so. I realized that if this was what God wanted us to do, He needed to speak to her as clearly as He had spoken to me. I knew it would be better for me to pray that she would hear from God than it would be to force the issue. So that's the way I prayed. And one afternoon a few weeks later, she sensed a clear leading from God that we were to make that move.

God makes it clear that our obedience to Him is vitally important to our spiritual health. He says that it's better than sacrifice. One of the most comforting things in my marriage is to know that my wife is walking in obedience to God. With that obedience comes a settled peace not only for my wife, but which gives a sense of well-being to our entire family. I know it inspires our children as well to walk in obedience to God. God can speak profoundly into each of our lives and give us a great sense of purpose when we seek Him and walk in obedience to what He wants. I pray for my wife to forsake anything that stands in the way of her obeying God. Not only do I want to pray that for her, but I want to personally model that to her as well.

PRAYER POWER

Lord, I pray that You would enable (<u>wife's name</u>) to live in total obedience to Your laws and Your ways. Help her to see where her thoughts and actions are not lined up with Your directions as to how she is to live. Help her to hear Your instructions, and give her the desire to do what You ask. Remind her to confess any error quickly, and enable her to take the steps of obedience she needs to take.

I know that one of the consequences for not living in obedience to Your ways is a sense of distance from You. Keep my wife from doing anything that separates her from the fullness of Your presence and Your love. Show her where she is not living in obedience, and help her to do what she needs to do. Your Word says, "He who obeys instruction guards his life" (Proverbs 19:16 NIV). Bless her mind, emotions, and will as she takes steps of obedience. Give her the confidence that comes from knowing she has just obeyed You.

Lord, You have said that "out of the overflow of the heart the mouth speaks" (Matthew 12:34 NIV). Fill my wife's heart with Your love, peace, and joy this day so that it overflows in her words. May Your Spirit control her tongue so that everything she speaks brings life. Help her to say as David did, "I have resolved that my mouth will not sin" (Psalm 17:3 NIV).

Lord, Your Word says, "No good thing will He withhold from those who walk uprightly" (Psalm 84:11). I pray that my wife will walk uprightly and that You will pour out Your blessings upon her. Especially bless her with the peace and long life You speak of in Your Word (Proverbs 3:1,2). I pray this day that my wife will walk in obedience to You and that You will reward her with an abundance of good things. Let the words of her mouth and the meditation of her heart be always acceptable in Your sight, O Lord, our strength and our Redeemer (Psalm 19:14).

POWER TOOLS

DO NOT FORGET MY LAW, BUT LET YOUR HEART KEEP MY COMMANDS; FOR LENGTH OF DAYS AND LONG LIFE AND PEACE THEY WILL ADD TO YOU. LET NOT MERCY AND TRUTH FORSAKE YOU; BIND THEM AROUND YOUR NECK, WRITE THEM ON THE TABLET OF YOUR HEART.

PROVERBS 3:1-3

SHE OPENS HER MOUTH WITH WISDOM, AND ON HER TONGUE IS THE LAW OF KINDNESS.

PROVERBS 31:26

HE WHO GUARDS HIS MOUTH PRESERVES HIS LIFE, BUT HE WHO OPENS WIDE HIS LIPS SHALL HAVE DESTRUCTION.

PROVERBS 13:3

THE PATH OF THE JUST IS LIKE THE SHINING SUN, THAT SHINES EVER BRIGHTER UNTO THE PERFECT DAY.

PROVERBS 4:18

WHO CAN FIND A VIRTUOUS WIFE? FOR HER WORTH IS FAR ABOVE RUBIES.

PROVERBS 31:10

CHAPTER TWENTY

HER FUTURE

I used to follow the stock market to see which companies were doing well and which ones were not. "Look at that," I'd say to myself. "If I had bought stock in this company I would have made so much money by now." I was great at picking stocks, but because I didn't invest anything I never made any money. It wasn't until I learned to invest something that I saw good returns.

The same is true for our future. When we invest in it wisely, we see greater dividends. However, unlike the stock market, when we *don't* invest anything, we can still lose. And those losses can be devastating.

The most profitable way to invest in the future is to pray. That way you can never lose. God promises to give us a future and a good reason to have hope, but we have to pray about it (Jeremiah 29:11). Your prayers for your wife's future are an investment that is guaranteed to reap benefits for the rest of your lives together.

Women can get very fearful about the future. It's probably because we feel quite vulnerable at times. A woman's most common fears about the future are over losing a child, becoming seriously ill or disabled, losing her husband, being alone, not being able to defend herself against an assailant, having no purpose or relevance, not being attractive, not being able to support herself, or not being needed. If her fears get to the point where she's afraid she doesn't have a future worth living, she can become confused, overwhelmed, and hopeless. Only the truth of what God says about who she is and why she's here can set her free from all that.

God says that your wife is His child (John 1:12) and she will never be alone (Matthew 28:20) or forsaken (Hebrews 13:5). She will always be loved (John 15:9), and she will live a victorious life (Romans 8:37). And everything that happens in her life will work together for good (Romans 8:28). Pray for your wife to believe that the things God says about her future are true.

WHEN YOUR WIFE IS IN MINISTRY

Having a wife in ministry requires much prayer from you. That means if your wife is serving the Lord by teaching, touching, or speaking into the lives and hearts of people in some way, it is crucial that she have your prayer covering. Whether she is singing to thousands of people, or teaching five children in a Sunday school class, or telling her elderly neighbor on the corner about the Lord, she needs your prayers. Whether she is so high-profile that people all over the country know her, or her ministry is one-on-one and the only person who knows the true extent of what she does for the kingdom of God is you, she needs your prayers. Without them she is the target of an enemy who is out to destroy her. The more powerfully the Lord is using her, the greater Satan's plans for her destruction. Don't ever underestimate the significance of your prayers for her. God will hear them. They will save her life and secure her future.

If *you* are in ministry, your wife may be the enemy's target just because she is at your side helping you with what

God is calling *you* to do. The devil will try to destroy *you* by destroying *her*. Show me a married man who is powerfully doing the Lord's work, and I'll show you a wife who has probably been attacked in some way by the enemy. If you and your wife are working *together* in ministry, that is more of a threat than the realm of darkness can bear. The enemy will pull out all the stops to see you both brought down. Be prepared by praying for one another daily, and have other strong believers covering you as well.

THE WISDOM TO GET THERE

One of the most important things your wife needs for the future is the wisdom to get there. Life can quickly get out of control and we can get off the path when we don't have wisdom and revelation from God. Your wife needs wisdom with finances, wisdom to distinguish between truth and lies, wisdom to know whether someone is trustworthy, wisdom to do the right thing, and wisdom to be at the right place at the right time. The perfect woman in the Bible was filled with wisdom, but that doesn't happen without prayer (Proverbs 31:26).

Most of a woman's decisions have to be made quickly, throughout the day. She needs to have the wisdom of the Lord in order to be able to make those decisions well. "If any of you lacks wisdom, let him ask of God, who gives to all liberally and without reproach, and it will be given to him" (James 1:5). If you ask God for wisdom, discernment, and understanding on behalf of your wife, she will be given the knowledge of God. Knowledge will help her to see who she is in the Lord. Wisdom will get her where she needs to go. What more does she need for her future?

When you have wisdom, discernment, understanding, and the knowledge of God, you don't have to worry about the future. I used to be despairing about mine because all I could ever see was my circumstances at the moment. But one day Pastor Jack Hayford said to me, "Don't let where you are become a prophecy of where you're going to stay."

Don't you love that? If your life isn't the way you want it to be right now, that doesn't mean it's always going to be that way. We women have a tendency to fear that things will never change.

Pastor Jack also said, "Don't judge your future by the people who are betting you don't have one."

We don't have to be concerned about whatever terrible thing someone might have predicted for our future. We don't have to worry about what the newspaper, the stock market, the neighbor next door, the guy at work, or Aunt Bessie, has said about our future. We just need to know what *God* says about it.

God says we need to have a vision. So we must ask Him for it. But getting a vision from God for our future doesn't mean He is going to reveal all the details of what's ahead. He only promises to reveal *Himself* to us, when we seek Him. That's because He doesn't want us to know the future—He wants us to know *Him. He* is our future. When we know *Him*, He guides us into the future He has for us.

So praying for your wife to have a vision for her life doesn't mean she's going to know all that's ahead for her. It just means that she'll see that she *does* have a future and that it is *good*. And that is enough.

The future is so uncertain that, even when things are going well, we can never get too cocky about it. Everything can change in one moment, and then our lives are forever different. That's because the enemy never stops making plans for our future. We have to be continually watchful in prayer to make certain that our future is securely in *God's* hands so *His* plans will prevail.

As you pray for your wife's future, remember that it's *your* future too. That's because your future is not independent of hers, nor is hers separate from yours. They are intertwined. This is the reason that the prayers you pray for your wife are guaranteed to yield a return that will make you secure for the rest of your lives. If you keep investing in your wife's future with prayer, I guarantee that your lives are going to be rich with blessings from God.

SHE SAYS...

Please pray for your wife that:

1. She will not fear the future.
2. She will have wisdom in all things.
3. She will have a vision and hope for her future.
4. She will be able to make quick decisions wisely.
5. She will not listen to lies of the enemy about her future.
6. She will bear fruit into old age.
7. Her future will be secure.

HE SAYS...
BY EDDIE L. LONG

Bishop Long is the senior pastor of New Birth Missionary Baptist Church in Lithonia, Georgia. He and his wife, Vanessa, have been married for 11 years, and they have four children.

My wife is regarded as a mother to many people—more than 22,000 parishioners in our church at last count. She is an articulate, educated, kind, demure, God-fearing lady who does not seek the limelight. But Vanessa's destiny is tied to mine, and because she is my wife, many times she winds up at center stage where all eyes are upon her. She has an innate ability to handle any situation with grace, and I continually pray that she will hear clearly from God and follow His destiny for her life.

I have witnessed several changes in my wife over the years. She has stretched out her hand and addressed issues that touch the women of our congregation and others connected to our ministry. She has decided to get to the heart of women's issues by dealing with grassroots problems. I believe the answers to my prayers for my wife are seen each day as she helps heal the broken hearts and homes of those she touches. Without prayer, I don't believe the Heart to Heart Women's Ministry under her leadership would touch the hearts of women and change the lives of families worldwide as it does today.

I will not take any credit for God's plan or the prayers that have been prayed by our family and friends, but I know I pray for my wife. As her husband, I believe that my prayers help sanctify her for God's use. Prayer changes things. Prayer brings an increased measure of God's power. Much prayer, much power; little prayer, little power; no prayer, no power.

I continue to pray for my wife while reaping the benefits, because she is a blessing to all who have the good fortune to know her. I know that as God is ongoingly magnified in her life, she will continue to grow in glory. My wife is my glory, a gift from God. Praying for her in turn affects my life as we grow together in Christ.

"I love the LORD, because He has heard my voice and my supplications. Because He has inclined His ear to me, therefore I will call upon Him as long as I live" (Psalm 116:2).

PRAYER POWER

Lord, I pray for (<u>wife's name</u>) to have total peace about the past, present, and future of her life. Give her a vision for her future that makes her certain she is safe in Your hands. Keep her, and the people she loves, protected from the plans of the evil one. Free her completely from the past so that nothing interferes with the future You have for her. Help her to see her future from Your perspective and not believe any lies of the enemy about it. May she trust Your promise that the plans You have for her are for good and not evil, to give her a future and a hope (Jeremiah 29:11 NIV). Give her confidence that the future is something she never has to fear.

Lord, I pray that You would give (<u>wife's name</u>) wisdom in all things. When she has to make any decision, I pray that You, Holy Spirit, will guide her. Give her wisdom in her work, travels, relationships, and finances. Bless her with the discernment to distinguish the truth from a lie. May she have the contentment, longevity, enjoyment, vitality, riches, and happiness that Your Word says are there for those who find wisdom (Proverbs 3:16-18). May she also find protection, grace, rest, freedom from fear, and confidence in You (Proverbs 3:21-26). Take my wife from glory to glory and strength to strength as she learns to depend on Your wisdom and not lean on her own understanding.

For the decisions we must make together, give us wisdom to make them in unity. Specifically I pray for (<u>name a decision you must make together</u>). Help us to know Your will in this matter. I pray that we will make godly choices and decisions that are pleasing to You.

I pray that (<u>wife's name</u>) will be planted in Your house and flourish in Your courts. May the fruit of her life be seen every year, and even into old age may she be fresh and flourishing (Psalm 92:13,14). Bless her with long life, and when she comes to the end of her life, may it not be one moment before Your chosen time. Let that transition also be attended with peace and joy, and the absence of suffering. Let it be said of her that she was Your light to the world around her.

I say to (<u>wife's name</u>) this day, "You are complete in Him" (Colossians 2:10). I am confident that "He who has begun a good work in you will complete it until the day of Jesus Christ" (Philippians 1:6). "Arise, shine; for your light has come! And the glory of the LORD is risen upon you" (Isaiah 60:1).

POWER TOOLS

EYE HAS NOT SEEN, NOR EAR HEARD, NOR HAVE ENTERED
INTO THE HEART OF MAN THE THINGS WHICH GOD HAS PRE-
PARED FOR THOSE WHO LOVE HIM.

1 CORINTHIANS 2:9

THERE IS SURELY A FUTURE HOPE FOR YOU, AND YOUR HOPE
WILL NOT BE CUT OFF.

PROVERBS 23:18 NIV

KEEP SOUND WISDOM AND DISCRETION; SO THEY WILL BE
LIFE TO YOUR SOUL AND GRACE TO YOUR NECK. THEN YOU
WILL WALK SAFELY IN YOUR WAY, AND YOUR FOOT WILL NOT
STUMBLE. WHEN YOU LIE DOWN, YOU WILL NOT BE AFRAID;
YES, YOU WILL LIE DOWN AND YOUR SLEEP WILL BE SWEET.
DO NOT BE AFRAID OF SUDDEN TERROR, NOR OF TROUBLE
FROM THE WICKED WHEN IT COMES; FOR THE LORD WILL BE
YOUR CONFIDENCE, AND WILL KEEP YOUR FOOT FROM BEING
CAUGHT.

PROVERBS 3:21-26

HOUSES AND RICHES ARE AN INHERITANCE FROM FATHERS,
BUT A PRUDENT WIFE IS FROM THE LORD.

PROVERBS 19:14

I KNOW THE THOUGHTS THAT I THINK TOWARD YOU, SAYS
THE LORD, THOUGHTS OF PEACE AND NOT OF EVIL, TO GIVE
YOU A FUTURE AND A HOPE. THEN YOU WILL CALL UPON ME
AND GO AND PRAY TO ME, AND I WILL LISTEN TO YOU. AND
YOU WILL SEEK ME AND FIND ME, WHEN YOU SEARCH FOR
ME WITH ALL YOUR HEART.

JEREMIAH 29:11-13

About the Author

Stormie Omartian is an award-winning, bestselling author who personally connects with readers by sharing experiences and lessons that illustrate how God transforms lives when we trust Him, seek His will, and follow His lead in all circumstances. In her books and personal appearances, she demonstrates how to pray powerfully in order to find emotional wholeness, establish strong relationships, keep a marriage strong, survive tough times, and maintain a close relationship with God.

Raised in an abusive home, Stormie grew up with severe depression, anxiety, fear, and feelings of hopelessness and rejection. After seeking relief from her pain through drugs, alcohol, the occult, Eastern religions, and unhealthy relationships, Stormie planned to end her life. However, out of desperation, she agreed to go with a friend to meet Pastor Jack Hayford, who told her about Jesus and His amazing love for her. Stormie realized that she was separated from God, and the only way to bridge that separation was to receive Jesus as her Savior.

As Stormie grew in her faith, she found freedom from her depression, anxiety, and fear, and she began to learn about the power of prayer. Through speaking engagements in cities and churches across the United States, appearances on radio and television, and in her autobiography, *Stormie*, she shares her story of emotional healing and finding redemption in Christ.

She is also the bestselling author (more than 23 million copies sold) of The Power of a Praying® series, which includes *The Power of a Praying® Wife Devotional* and *The Power of Praying® for Your Adult Children*. Her many other books include *Just Enough Light for the Step I'm On, The Prayer That Changes Everything®, Praying the Bible into Your Life,* and *Lead Me, Holy Spirit*. Stormie and her husband, Michael, have been married more than 39 years and are the parents of two married children.

Stormie understands the tremendous sacrifice military families make for our country as her nephew is on his second deployment in Iraq. You can find out more about Stormie at www.stormieomartian.com.

Other resources available from
The 1687 Foundation

Books of Hope and Faith

***31 Days of Praise* by Ruth Myers, *also available in Spanish*.** Christians who long to experience God in a fresh, deeper way will treasure this powerful, personal praise guide. Every day for just one month, a Scripture-based devotion cultivates the "heart habit" of praise and worship. Readers will be amazed to discover how their lives can be *touched* and *changed* on a day-by-day, month-by-month basis. They will be gently inspired to appreciate and adore the Lord in all things—yes, even in the midst of pain, disappointment, and heartache. A deeper intimacy with God, and a greater love for Him, is the sure result. Come into His presence with praise.

***31 Days of Prayer* by Ruth Myers, *also available in Spanish*.** God invites us—*welcomes us*—into the high privilege of talking and working with Him. *31 Days of Prayer* shows you how to enjoy that privilege and begin an incredible prayer adventure. You'll discover in new ways that prayer is the slender nerve that moves the mighty hand of God. This is the perfect book to lead you in prayer for a full month—or many months—and help you create a prayer habit that lasts a lifetime. Rise above earthbound living…and into a new awareness of the Lord's delightful presence!

***Karla Faye Tucker Set Free: Life and Faith on Death Row* by Linda Strom,** Karla Faye Tucker, the first woman executed in Texas in over one hundred years, became an evangelist for Christ during her fourteen-year imprisonment on Death Row. This is the story of Karla's spiritual journey, the women and men she reached, and the God who offers redemption and hope to the hardest of hearts.

***Fruit Happens!* by Michael Christopher**
Fruit happens when you spend time with God! *Fruit Happens!* also features one of the most exciting characters you might ever meet. His name is Dellie O'Shea, and his game is "over the top" in every possible way.

Dellie O'Shea is not someone who sits on the sidelines and watches the world pass by. He's a young man who puts his best instincts into action, especially those he gets directly from God. Along the way he learns what the "Fruits of the Spirit" are all about, by saving the life of another even as those same spiritual fruits grow and develop within himself.

He's also a Very Special Person in other ways as well—but you'll have to read his story to find out what they are!

Golden Turnabout by **Michael Christopher**
Golden Turnabouts happen when you see with more than your eyes! This is the second in a series, featuring most of the same fascinating characters you've met before—including Dellie O'Shea! This time Dellie makes a new friend who seems to be slightly different from anyone else he's ever known. And maybe a little more prickly, too.

But things aren't always the way they first appear. Sometimes we judge a little too quickly, based on what we see on the outside before we have a chance to look a little deeper. And sometimes when we least expect it, others "do unto us" in ways that change our world for the better, even as Christ Himself would have us "do unto them."

Psalm 91: God's Umbrella of Protection by **Peggy Joyce Ruth**, *also available in Spanish.*
Do the latest statistics on cancer, heart disease, and other medical conditions send a chill down your spine? Do thoughts of terrorist attacks and chemical warfare cause your heart to skip a beat? What about all the natural disasters that strike in unexpected places? Indeed—do you sometimes wonder if there is any safe haven anywhere in the world in which you might someday want to hide? If any of these things have ever troubled you, this can be one of the most important books you will ever read! In Psalm 91, the author's highly revealing, biblically based examination of the blessings God promises will open your heart, strengthen your spirit, and revitalize every aspect of your life!

Psalm 91: God's Shield of Protection by **Peggy Joyce Ruth** and **Angelia Ruth Shum**

My Own Psalm 91 by **Peggy Joyce Ruth**, *also available in Spanish.*
—Children's version.

The Cross Pin
(shown mounted on card)

To request books or cross pins, or for more information, please contact:

The 1687 Foundation
P.O. Box 1961, Sisters, OR 97759
Email: info@1687foundation.com
541.549.7600 tel•541.549.7603 fax